KU-438-876

How to Figure Out Company Accounts

Michael Brett

TEXERE

New York • London

Copyright © 2003 Michael Brett

Published by

TEXERE Publishing Limited
71–77 Leadenhall Street
London EC3A 3DE

Tel: +44 (0)20 7204 3644
Fax: +44 (0)20 7208 6701
www.etexere.co.uk

A subsidiary of

TEXERE LLC
55 East 52nd Street
New York, NY 10055

Tel: +1 (212) 317 5511
Fax: +1 (212) 317 5178
www.etexere.com

The right of Michael Brett to be identified as the author of this work has been asserted by him in accordance with the Copyright, Designs and Patents Act 1988.

All rights reserved.

No part of this publication may be reproduced, stored in a retrieval system or transmitted in any form or by any means including photocopying, electronic, mechanical, recording or otherwise, without the prior written permission of the right holders, application for which must be made to the publisher.

No responsibility can be accepted by the publisher for action taken as a result of information contained in this publication. Readers should take specific advice when dealing with specific situations.

TEXERE books may be purchased for educational, business, or sales promotional use. For more information please write to the Special Markets Department at the TEXERE London address.

Designed and project managed by Macfarlane Production Services, Markyate, Hertfordshire, England (e-mail: macfarl@aol.com).

A CIP catalogue record for this book is available from the British Library.

ISBN 1-58799-033-4

Printed and bound in Great Britain by Ashford Colour Press Ltd, Gosport, Hampshire.

This book is printed on acid-free paper responsibly manufactured from sustainable forestry, in which at least two trees are planted for each one used for paper production.

Contents

Contents

Part II Understanding the words   93

Acknowledgements

During the preparation of this book Antonia Oprita provided valuable suggestions and comment and picked up many of the inconsistencies. Susan Bevan read the completed manuscript and it has benefited from her suggested changes and corrections. I am extremely grateful to both of them. Any remaining errors are my own.

Cartoons by Nick Newman.

Introduction

Accounts are in the news and accountants are under scrutiny. Accounting fiddles at energy group Enron and communications giant WorldCom in the United States in 2001 and 2002 focused the spotlight on an aspect of business that rarely hits the headlines. The detailed figures with which companies record their performance and their financial strength are not normally regarded as sexy or worthy of comment outside the business pages. This time they were big news, contributing to a slump in share prices on world stock markets and even threatening to undermine the popularity of the business-orientated US President, George W. Bush.

People will be paying a lot more attention to company accounts in future. But accounts can be intimidating, particularly to those who do not often have to deal with them. They have their own language and conventions. Unless you understand some of this language, they may be totally incomprehensible; a meaningless jumble of figures.

This book sets out to explain the language of company accounts and it assumes no prior knowledge of the subject. It is therefore aimed at the person who faces a set of accounts for the first time and tries to make some sense out of the mass of facts and figures. However, even those who are familiar with basic accounting concepts may find it useful to remind themselves of what lies behind the welter of information that is provided nowadays in the report and accounts of companies whose shares are listed on a stock market.

In the past, companies have often been accused of providing too little information in their accounts. Today, the shareholder who receives annual accounts from a company he has invested in faces the opposite problem. There is arguably too much information. The sheer volume risks obscuring what is really relevant. In particular, companies are nowadays required to provide masses of information on the pay and perks of their directors, on their observance of various rules and codes of conduct, on their policies on a wide range of issues from environmental responsibility to employment of the disabled. While well intentioned, these requirements of the 'corporate governance' industry often swamp the relevant information about the company's performance and financial position. One major drinks company devotes nine pages of its report and accounts to details of directors' remuneration against three for the main financial accounts. It is not untypical.

In this book we chart a way through the annual report and accounts, explaining what is most directly relevant to the company's performance and prospects but also explaining the background to the mass of additional information that the reader will encounter. The principles of the accounts themselves are explained with the help of 'invented' examples, introducing one concept at a time and gradually building up to the full picture. The basic financial ratios, used by investors in particular, are also explained. Later in the book we turn more to questions of interpretation and analysis and introduce the accounts of a real company. Finally, we look at some of the more common ways that accounts may be 'fiddled'. And as an antidote to facts and figures, we also provide our own tongue-in-cheek interpretations of some of the phrases you might encounter from the pen of a company chairman or chief executive. The book rounds off with a comprehensive index and glossary.

Nobody can be certain that they will spot the next accounting scandal before the damage is done. After all, the accounting shenanigans at Enron and WorldCom eluded some of the best brains in the investment world for a considerable time. But a knowledge of the basic principles of company accounting will help you to spot some of the more common signs of future trouble in a company's accounts, as well as helping you to understand what the figures tell you about the performance and prospects of a business. When the stock market is bubbling and everybody is making a lot of money, few bother to read the small print of the accounts of companies they invest in. But the climate is likely to be very different after Enron and WorldCom and the trouble on world stock markets to which they contributed. A basic understanding of accounts is useful to all who have dealings with companies, including employees, trade unions and prospective pensioners. For investors it is perhaps the most useful weapon in their armoury.

How to use this book

Much of this book is concerned with the basic accounting items that you will come across in a company's published report and accounts. But before launching into this, read the brief following section **Some basic facts about companies**. This gives background information about companies in general and what information you can discover about them, which helps to set the scene for what comes later.

Next we move to the accounts themselves in the main part of the book: **Understanding the figures**. The approach needs a little explanation. We have assumed no existing knowledge of accounts, so the starting point is the first principles, which are illustrated one concept at a time. In each case an explanation is accompanied by an example, which is itself annotated. Because the published accounts of real companies contain so much information that may obscure the individual components, we have used simplified 'invented' examples to introduce one concept at a time and gradually build up to the full picture. These examples are not presented in quite the same format that you will find in a genuine set of published accounts. For a start, 'real' accounts normally give the figures for two years: the latest year and the previous one. The movements in the figures between the two years can tell you a lot about what is happening at the company, and we address this aspect later in the book. But the welter of figures can confuse the beginner so we have stuck to showing just one year's worth of figures in our basic examples.

We have also used colour to draw attention to the nature of the individual accounts items – something you again would not find in a real set of accounts. The basic convention we have used here is that things that the company owns or revenue that it earns are shown in light grey. Deductions for what the company owes or for expenses incurred are shown in red to distinguish them clearly. And though the full financial statement may be shown in the example, the figures under discussion in that section are shown in bold to draw attention to them. Again, you will not find this treatment in a set of published accounts.

We have called our first sample company SimpleCo, and the first part of the accounts section deals with the basic financial statements – profit and loss account, balance sheet and cash flow statement (see below) – of this company. It also explains how to calculate the basic accounts ratios that investors and others use when rating or comparing different companies.

We then turn to a slightly more complex company example – ComplexCo – to illustrate some of the more advanced features that crop up in many company accounts. Finally, various company examples are used to demonstrate the effect on a company's accounts of a number of operations such as share issues and takeovers. The possible effects of using different amounts of borrowed money are also illustrated.

Since the accounts examples are designed to introduce one concept at a time, it is better to work through them in sequence at the first reading, rather than dipping in and out. You may also find it helpful to have the published accounts of a real company by you as you work your way through. Thus you may see how the items we explain are likely to be presented in practice. Note that companies have the option nowadays of providing shareholders with a 'summary' report and accounts, though the shareholder has the right to require the full document. These summary accounts – sometimes disrespectfully referred to as 'Noddy' accounts – may omit much of the financial detail that you would need for a full understanding of the figures, so we advise avoiding them. It is the full report and accounts you should be looking at.

Our own examples are based on a smallish manufacturing business. Whereas the same principles hold good across most types of company, the shape of the accounts will vary with the nature of the business. A service company such as an advertising business, for example, may need very little in the way of tangible long-term assets since its real assets are its connections and expertise and the people who work for it. And the cash needs of a supermarket group are probably different from those of a manufacturing business. A supermarket group may be able to get cash in from selling products before it has to pay its own suppliers for them. Increased sales may thus generate cash, whereas most businesses find that expansion generates additional cash needs. Bear in mind differences of this sort when applying the basic principles to different types of business.

The report and accounts of any company, but particularly one listed on the stock exchange, contain a lot of information in addition to the basic financial statements. After dealing with the accounts themselves we then look in Part II, **Understanding the words**, at the additional useful information about the company that you should be able to find in one part or another of the document, including the notes to the accounts. We also explain the background to the other main topics that will be covered in the narrative sections of the report and accounts.

The next part, **What it all means**, turns from explanation to interpretation and suggests how a set of accounts should be approached. This is followed by Part IV, **Removing the veil**, which takes a real-life example of a company's accounts and illustrates what might be deduced from them.

Nobody should look at a set of accounts without bearing in mind that there are various ways the figures can be manipulated to present a favourable picture. This can vary from fairly harmless tweaking of the figures to outright falsification. So in Part IV, we look at some of the more common ways that figures may be presented to give a more favourable – or outright misleading – impression. And finally, since accounts can be a somewhat dry topic and company directors are prone to take themselves too seriously, we take a tongue-in-cheek look at what may lie behind some of the more familiar turns of phrase you might come across in a company's report and accounts.

The book is rounded off by a comprehensive **index and glossary** which points to sections of the text where items are explained and adds explanations of some terms which are not covered elsewhere.

Some basic facts about companies

Limited companies fall into two main types (we'll come to the significance of that word 'limited' in a moment). Companies whose shares or securities are traded on a market – plus a few others – need to be **public limited companies**. They have the initials **plc** after their name and there is a minimum share capital requirement. Other companies are simply **limited companies**, with **Ltd** after the name. The subsidiaries of public limited companies will normally be simple limited companies, unless their shares are traded separately in their own right.

The word 'limited' stands for **limited liability**. What it means is that the owners of the company cannot normally lose more money than they have put into the business. They are not personally responsible (as sole traders or partners in a partnership would be) for the debts of the company if these exceed its ability to pay. However, the owners of small businesses are often required by banks to give personal guarantees for loans to the company, which partly negates the protection offered by the limited liability structure.

Companies in England and Wales, whether public or private, are required to file information with the **Registrar of Companies**. The **Companies Registry** is headquartered in Cardiff, but there are branches in London and a few other major cities. The information that must be filed includes an **annual return** giving details of share capital, of the directors, the company secretary and the shareholders, the address of the registered office and a few other items. Changes (except to shareholdings) must be notified shortly after they occur. **Annual accounts** must also be filed. One other document that companies must keep up to date at the **Companies Registry** as well as at their own office is a **register of charges**, which shows what assets of the company (if any) are pledged as security for loans.

Information filed with the Companies Registry (usually known as **Companies House**) is available for inspection by the public on payment of a modest fee. This facility is used a great deal by credit agencies, who will report on a company's financial standing to those who might consider doing business with it.

As well as the information they are required to file at Companies House, companies are required to maintain certain information at their own offices. Obviously they have to maintain proper accounting records. But they are also required to maintain and constantly update a **register of shareholders**. Small companies are likely to keep this at their registered office. Large public companies probably farm out the business of maintaining the share register to professional **registrars**, who specialise in this business. Either way, members of the public have a right to inspect the share register, again on payment of a modest fee. Companies are also required to keep a register of their directors' interests in the company's share capital and note any changes rapidly. In the case of companies listed on the stock exchange, all dealings by directors in the company's own shares must also be notified to, and published by, the stock exchange. There is a **close season**, for a couple of months before the publication of the half-yearly and annual results, during which directors are not normally meant to deal in their company's shares.

Many aspects of the conduct of company affairs – including those mentioned in the previous paragraph – are regulated by law. The **Companies Acts** (of which the **Companies Act 1985** is the most recent comprehensive revision) set out the basic rules on directors' powers and responsibilities, and the rules to which companies themselves must conform. Among the more important items covered are issues of share capital, preparation and audit of accounts, conduct of shareholders' meetings and the like. These requirements normally apply to all companies. In addition, each company has its own 'constitution' set out in documents known as its **Memorandum** and **Articles of Association**. These set out the company's objects and the specific rules that will govern a number of aspects of its operations.

Companies that wish to **market** their shares to investors for the first time – probably via a stock market launch – are required to produce a **prospectus**, providing a great deal of financial and accounting information, together with details of the people who run the company. The prospectus is a document backed by the force of law, and issuing an inaccurate or false prospectus is a serious offence.

Public companies that want their shares traded on the **main market** of the **London Stock Exchange** are required to observe a **Listing Agreement** (now administered by the **Financial Services Authority** or **FSA**). This imposes standards in a number of areas, particularly in the provision of information to shareholders. This information is considerably more than what is required of all companies by the Companies Acts. For a start, companies will be required to publish half-yearly performance figures as well as the annual figures required by law. These companies are therefore described as **listed** on the stock exchange. In addition, the London Stock Exchange operates a second-tier market known as the **Alternative Investment Market** or **AIM**. Companies whose shares are traded on AIM observe a slightly more relaxed set of rules than those imposed by the full listing agreement. They should not therefore be described as **listed companies**, but are probably referred to as **quoted** or **traded** on the market.

The owners of a company are its **shareholders** or '**members**'. In the case of small private companies, the shareholders may also be the **directors** of the company. But these are two separate functions, even if they may be exercised by the same people. The shareholders, acting together, have the power to appoint and dismiss directors and a number of other powers. But the directors run the company and are legally responsible for its actions. Directors do not need to hold shares in the company (though many do) unless required by the company's constitution. Nor do shareholders need to be directly involved in a company's management. Large listed companies may have tens of thousands of shareholders who may or may not cast their votes on the appointment of directors and similar matters, but who are not otherwise involved in the running of the company.

With most companies, each ordinary share carries one **vote** which may be exercised by the shareholder (other classes of share capital may carry votes only in particular circumstances). This is not a universal rule. Some companies have different classes of ordinary shares, some of which carry more votes than others. Or there may be voting ordinary shares and non-voting ordinary (the latter carrying no votes at all). But the London Stock Exchange nowadays generally frowns on differential voting arrangements, at least for fully listed companies.

Most companies of a sufficient size to have their shares traded on a stock exchange are in fact **groups** of companies consisting of a **parent company** and **subsidiary companies** (companies controlled by the parent). In **consolidated** or **group accounts**, the figures of all these companies are lumped together as if they were a single entity. The accounts discussed in this book are consolidated accounts, and we have used the terms 'company' and 'group' pretty much interchangeably. Unless the context dictates otherwise, references to 'company' should be taken as referring to the group.

Part I

Understanding the figures

What is a company report and accounts?

The annual report and accounts is the main document you rely on for regular information about a company. But in the case of a company whose shares are traded on a stock exchange it is by no means the only one. Half-yearly and annual profit announcements, documents giving details of share issues and documents issued in the course of a takeover battle will all provide valuable information about a company's affairs.

The annual report and accounts is different, however, because it supplies much of the routine information that you need to track the company's progress.

The **profit and loss account** that it contains provides the annual scoreboard for the company's operations, underlining success or failure.

It also incorporates a **balance sheet**: an annual statement of everything the company owns and everything the company owes. This is an invaluable picture of a company's financial strengths and weaknesses.

The main **financial statements** (profit and loss account, **cash flow statement** and balance sheet) are by no means the only things that the annual report and accounts contains. In fact, they probably occupy only a small proportion of the document. Supplementing them is a wealth of information required by law, by stock exchange regulations, by codes of practice and by the need to explain many of the figures appearing in the financial statements. Much of this information appears in the **notes to the accounts** which are usually a great deal lengthier than the financial statements themselves.

In addition, the report and accounts almost certainly contains a considerable volume of narrative material. This will probably include:

- a statement by the chairman
- a review of the company's operations over the year

- a review of its finances and
- a number of specific statements on aspects of the company's policies.

For much of this narrative material there is no fixed format. Different companies group it and present it in different ways. At best it can put flesh on the bare figures of the financial statements and help towards an understanding of the company. At worst and – fortunately – rarely, it can be designed to mislead or to mask serious problems.

Besides recording past performance, the report and accounts can provide a pointer to a company's likely success or failure, to its stability and even to its life expectancy.

The **report and accounts** is the document in which the company's directors account to the owners – the **shareholders** or technically the **members** – for their stewardship of the company and show the results of that stewardship over the year.

The accounts that the directors present to shareholders need to be examined by a firm of independent accountants – the **auditors** who report whether or not they give a **true and fair view** of the company's affairs. If the auditors are watchful, it is difficult for the directors to pull the wool over the shareholders' eyes, even should they wish to. The **auditors' report** to shareholders is an important element of the report and accounts.

The auditors' primary duty is to give a view on the financial statements and the explanatory notes that accompany them. The auditors are also meant to check what the directors say about the company's performance to make sure it is not inconsistent with the figures. But they may sometimes be a little less rigorous here.

It is a requirement of company law that shareholders should receive the report and accounts at least three weeks before the company's **annual** general meeting (agm), which they are entitled to attend. The notice calling the agm will normally accompany the report and accounts, or may be printed in the document itself.

At the annual general meeting shareholders will be asked to vote on a number of resolutions relating to the report and accounts (in practice they also have the option of a postal vote). Other items of business may also be brought forward at the agm.

The main financial statements

There are three main **financial statements** in a set of annual accounts. It is important to understand what each of them sets out to show. These three financial statements are: the **profit and loss account**; the **cash flow statement**; and the **balance sheet**.

The profit and loss account and the cash flow statement summarise the company's experiences over its financial year. The balance sheet is different in that it provides a snapshot of what the company owns and what it owes – its **assets** and its **liabilities** – on one particular day: the last day of the company's financial year.

Companies may choose whatever **financial year** they like for the purpose of producing their accounts. It does not have to coincide with the calendar year or the tax year. In the event, year-ends of 31 December and 31 March (the latter corresponding roughly with the tax year, which runs to 5 April) are popular. But there are plenty of companies with year-ends at 30 June or 30 September and other dates in between. You may end your financial year on 1 April if your sense of humour points you that way.

Whatever year-end is chosen, the profit and loss account and cash flow statement normally cover the twelve months up to that date. But this is not invariably the case. A company might decide to change its year-end from 31 December to 31 March, in which case it would probably produce accounts covering a fifteen-month period to 31 March when it first makes the change.

The **profit and loss account** is probably the most familiar and the most quoted of the financial statements. It records the result of the year's trading: what profit or loss the company made over the period as a whole. It gives the profit or loss figure both before and after the **corporation tax** on profits that companies must pay. Press headlines focus on the profit or the loss that a company has made during the year, as this is the point of most immediate interest to investors. The profit and loss account summarises the result of the year's operations, but in doing so it will not necessarily give the full picture. Do not automatically take a profit figure at face value. It can be manipulated in various ways. You need to look more carefully to see the source and 'quality' of the profits. Suppose, for instance, a company made a loss of £6om in the first six months of its financial year but, following remedial action, earned a profit of £4om in the final six months. The profit and loss account for the year as a whole would show a loss of £2om, obscuring the fact that the company was trading profitably by its year-end.

Profit is also an **accounting convention** rather than an absolute truth. There's room for an element of interpretation and opinion in what constitutes a profit. This is where the **cash flow statement** comes in. This records the cash actually received and disbursed over the year, where opinion plays a far smaller part.

A company may have made a profit in accounting terms during the year but still have seen more cash flowing out than in. This is important – companies can go bust if they run out of cash, whatever the profit figures may appear to show. The **cash flow statement** is your best guide as to whether the company is generating cash or leaking cash – and the effect this is having on its borrowings. So why does cash flow often give a different picture from profit? Take an example. A company earns interest of £1om during the year on money it has lent. This interest would count towards its profit. But perhaps it has not received the interest by the year-end. In other words, income and expenditure are treated on an **accruals** basis: as they are earned or incurred and not necessarily as they are received or paid. Thus, the £10m of accrued interest that was included in profits would not be included in cash flow, since it is not cash that has been received. Indeed, there may be no guarantee that it ever will be received. Profit is theoretical. Cash is a fact.

The **balance sheet** shows the company's assets and liabilities – including what cash it has – on a particular date. Though this is useful in helping to establish a company's financial strength, remember that the position might have looked significantly different a month earlier or a month later. It is a snapshot that catches only one particular moment in time.

What the **balance sheet** does provide is the best guide as to the soundness (or otherwise) of the company's finances. It shows you what the company owns. But since it also shows what the company owes, it allows you to see how much the company relies on borrowed money and how much of the money it uses is its own (i.e. shareholders') money. Too great a reliance on borrowed money is one of the main reasons why companies go bust.

The profit and loss account basics

As the name suggests, the **profit and loss account** shows what profit or loss the company made during the year and, as we have seen, profit is not necessarily the same thing as cash flow.

The example opposite is simplified to show the essential features. For clarity we have shown income in light grey and deductions from that income in red. In practice companies show two years' worth of figures in their accounts: those for the latest year and for the previous one. To avoid confusing with too much detail, we have stuck to one year's worth here.

The starting point is **turnover** (sometimes also described as **sales**). This is the value of goods and services sold by the company during the year exclusive of value added tax (VAT). Let us assume that SimpleCo is in the business of manufacturing and marketing garden gnomes and other garden products. The rise or fall in turnover from one year to the other can give an indication of whether SimpleCo's business is increasing or decreasing. But be a little careful. Turnover could rise simply because the SimpleCo had raised its selling prices during the year or because it had bought another business whose turnover was then lumped in with its own.

From the value of the goods or services the company sold during the year we have to deduct the costs of producing and selling them. These cost items would of course include raw materials: the plastics or clay that the company uses to manufacture its gnomes, the paints with which they are coloured, and so on. They would also include wages, energy costs, administration, distribution and selling costs, possibly rent of buildings and similar costs. In addition they would incorporate a provision to cover the wearing out and ultimate replacement of plant and machinery – the **depreciation** allowance. These costs are not normally shown in detail on the **face of the accounts** (i.e. on the profit and loss account itself), though some will be itemised in the notes to the accounts.

After deducting all these costs except interest on borrowed money we arrive at **operating profit**. This is one of the main definitions of profit that will be quoted by investment analysts, financial journalists and others who comment on company performance.

Next we have to deduct **interest payable**. These are the interest charges that the company clocked up during the year on the **borrowed money** it used (often described as **borrowings**, **loans** or **debt**). The interest payable may be shown **net**: i.e. after deducting any interest due to the company on its cash balances.

What is left after interest charges is the **profit before tax** (often called **pre-tax profit**). This is the most widely used measure of a company's profits. It shows what is left after deducting the main costs except the **corporation tax** that companies pay on their profits.

Next the corporation tax, taken at 30%, must be deducted to give, in our example, the **net profit after tax**. There may in practice be one or two more deductions that have to be made at this point – we will deal with these later. But assume for simplicity that no further deductions need to be made. This net profit after tax is therefore the profit that belongs to the ordinary shareholders of SimpleCo, often described as **earnings**.

Whatever profit a company earns *belongs* to its **ordinary shareholders** after all charges have been made. This is a very important principle. It does not, however, mean that all this profit is necessarily paid out to shareholders. More often, the company will pay only part of its earnings to its owners – the shareholders – by way of **dividend**. In our example the dividends absorb £3m of the £7m profit. The remaining £4m of profit – usually called **retained profit** – is ploughed back into the business to help in financing its growth. But remember that, even though this retained profit has not been paid out to shareholders, it belongs to them. It becomes part of the shareholders' money or **shareholders' funds** employed in the business.

Turnover or **sales** is the value in money terms of the goods and services sold by the company to third parties during the year. It does not normally include taxes, such as VAT, that may have been paid on those sales

Operating profit is what the company earned after charging all the costs of production but before paying interest on borrowed money and before charging any exceptional 'one-off' costs.

Interest payable shows the cost of interest on borrowed money, perhaps after deducting any interest that the company received. It is not necessarily the same as **interest paid**, which is what the cash flow statement would show.

Profit before tax is the most commonly quoted measure of a company's profits. But sometimes, when it includes large 'one-off' items, it may be a little misleading (see later).

Corporation tax shows the tax payable to the government, based on the year's profits but with some allowances.

Net profit after tax is the profit that has been earned for shareholders after everyone else – including the tax man – has had his take. It is often referred to as **earnings**.

Dividends shows the amount of profit that is paid to the shareholders, usually in two chunks: an **interim dividend** part way through the year and a **final dividend** after the year has ended.

Retained profit is the portion of the year's profit that is ploughed back into the business to help finance its growth. It forms part of the **shareholders' funds** of the company.

SimpleCo plc

CONSOLIDATED PROFIT AND LOSS ACCOUNT FOR THE YEAR ENDED 31 DECEMBER

	£m
TURNOVER	100
OPERATING PROFIT	12
less INTEREST PAYABLE	2
PROFIT BEFORE TAX	10
less CORPORATION TAX	3
NET PROFIT AFTER TAX	7
less DIVIDENDS	3
RETAINED PROFIT	4

Useful ratios to measure performance

A number of **ratios** that can tell you something useful about a company's performance can be worked out from the profit and loss account. One of the most important is: how much of what the company earns from selling its products or services ends up as profit? This ratio can be calculated using either the **operating profit** or the **profit before tax** (pre-tax profit).

Look again at our example. SimpleCo sells goods and services worth £100m in a year. After all costs except interest have been met, £12m of this £100m comes through as operating profit. The £12m is 12% of SimpleCo's £100m turnover, so we could say that the company has **operating profit margins** or **operating margins** of 12%.

The same sum can be done with the profit before tax. The £10m pre-tax profit represents 10% of SimpleCo's sales, to give a **pre-tax profit margin** or **pre-tax margin** of 10%. These profit margins are not greatly informative by themselves, but they tell you rather more when you compare their progress from one year to the next or when you compare them with the corresponding figures for other companies in the same line of business.

If margins have risen, you might conclude that SimpleCo has succeeded in cutting its costs or that it has managed to raise its prices. If margins have fallen you might reckon that the company has come under competitive pressure, which has forced its prices down or prevented them from rising to match increased costs.

Another ratio you will certainly look at is the relationship between the company's operating profit before interest charges and the size of these interest charges. In our example, interest charges absorb £2m of the operating profit of £12m. You could express this as 'interest costs are covered 6 times (£12m divided by £2m) by profits before interest'. Another way of saying this is '**interest cover** is 6 times'.

Why is this important? The interest cover figure gives a good indication of whether the cost of paying interest on borrowed money is likely to be a dangerous burden on the company. In our example, profits would have to fall quite a long way before they ceased to cover the interest. But if the interest cover were a great deal lower, you might wonder how safe SimpleCo would be if profits fell sharply.

Remember that a company may be forced to close if it is unable to pay the interest on money it has borrowed. Its ability to pay interest is not simply a function of the profit it earns in a year. It also depends on the cash that the company has available. But a company which consistently fails to generate enough profit to pay its interest costs is likely to run out of cash pretty quickly.

The ratio between available profits and interest charges may, as we've seen, be presented in a number of different ways. However expressed, a company's **income gearing** (the relationship between profits and interest charges) is a vital tool.

SimpleCo plc

CONSOLIDATED PROFIT AND LOSS ACCOUNT FOR THE YEAR ENDED 31 DECEMBER

	£m
TURNOVER	100
OPERATING PROFIT	12
less INTEREST PAYABLE	2
PROFIT BEFORE TAX	10
less CORPORATION TAX	3
NET PROFIT AFTER TAX	7
less DIVIDENDS	3
RETAINED PROFIT	4

The operating profit expressed as a percentage of turnover gives you the company's **operating profit margin** or **operating margin**. In this case it is 12%.

The profit before tax expressed as a percentage of turnover gives you the **pre-tax profit margin** or **pre-tax margin**. In this case it is 10%.

The ratio between profits before interest (**operating profit**) and the interest charge gives you the **interest cover**. In this case interest cover is 6 times, arrived at by dividing interest charges of £2m into operating profits of £12m. Interest cover or **income gearing** can give an indication of the level of risk built into the company's financial structure.

Ratios that the stock market uses

The **ratios** that we have looked at so far are those that tell you something about a company's trading performance and financial strength. But there are other ratios derived from the profit and loss account that are more directly relevant to the stock market standing of the company and the price of its shares.

The starting point is the figure for **net profit after tax**, from which there are no further deductions except dividends in our example, and which we saw is often referred to as **earnings**.

In our example SimpleCo has earnings of £7m. This is the total amount of earnings available for all shareholders. But how much profit does SimpleCo earn for each share? We can find out simply by dividing the £7m earnings figure by the number of **ordinary shares** in issue.

Let us assume that SimpleCo has 20,000,000 ordinary shares in issue. Convert the £7m into pence by multiplying by 100, then divide the result by the 20m shares. The result is 35p. In other words, our company earns 35p after tax for each share in issue. This figure is usually referred to as the **earnings per share** or **eps** and it forms the basis of an important investment ratio: the **price–earnings ratio**. We will look at this later.

The growth or decline in earnings per share from one year to the next is one of the best indicators of a company's performance, even though it might sometimes be manipulated in the short run by an unscrupulous management. It is a better guide than the pre-tax profit figure for the following reason. If SimpleCo bought another company, its pre-tax profits and profits after tax might be swollen by the profits of the newcomer. But suppose SimpleCo paid for the newcomer by creating and issuing new shares, which were swapped for the shares of the newcomer. In this case the number of shares in issue goes up. The earnings for each of this increased number of shares might not have risen at all. And it is the earnings per share that give an indication of dividend-paying ability.

This leads to another ratio: **dividend cover**, which provides a rough and ready indication of the safety of the dividend. SimpleCo paid a £3m dividend out of earnings of £7m. In other words, it could have paid this dividend 2.3 times out of the available earnings. So dividend cover is 2.3 times.

Dividends are usually expressed as an amount per share. To arrive at the **dividend per share**, multiply the £3m cost of the dividend by 100 to convert it to pence, then divide by the 20m shares in issue. The result is 15p, which is the dividend paid on each share.

Provided the shareholder is liable only to basic rate income tax, he does not have to pay anything more on the 15p dividend that he receives, though higher-rate taxpayers will be liable for additional tax.

The **earnings** – the **net profit after tax** in our examples – is divided by the number of shares in issue to calculate the **earnings per share** or **eps**. We have assumed there are 20m shares in issue, so the eps works out at 35p.

The rise or fall in this figure is a useful measure of how good a job the company is doing for its shareholders but there are two qualifications. Managements may find it possible to manipulate the eps in the short run. And the earnings on which it is based may include exceptional **one-off profit** items that may not be repeated. We will look at this problem later.

The **net profit after tax** or **earnings** gives an indication of the maximum size of **dividend** that the company could have paid out of its profits. The £7m of earnings would have allowed dividends of 2.3 times the £3m actually paid, so dividend cover is 2.3 times. When a company pays dividends which exceed the available earnings, you talk of an **uncovered dividend**.

Dividends are paid out of profits that have borne corporation tax and some of this tax is deemed to have been paid on behalf of the shareholders who receive the dividends. However, shareholders who are not liable to tax cannot claim back this tax paid on their behalf.

Earnings per share or **eps** are the company's earnings after tax divided by the number of shares in issue. **Dividends per share** are the total amount paid in dividends divided by the number of shares in issue.

SimpleCo plc

CONSOLIDATED PROFIT AND LOSS ACCOUNT FOR THE YEAR ENDED 31 DECEMBER

	£m
TURNOVER	100
OPERATING PROFIT	12
less INTEREST PAYABLE	2
PROFIT BEFORE TAX	10
less CORPORATION TAX	3
NET PROFIT AFTER TAX	7
less DIVIDENDS	3
RETAINED PROFIT	4
Earnings per share	35p
Dividends per share (assuming 20m shares in issue)	15p

What the company owns and what it owes

The **balance sheet** contained in the annual report is a snapshot of the company on the last day of its financial year. It shows everything that the company *owns* and everything that it *owes* on that particular date: its **assets** and its **liabilities**. As such, it is an invaluable guide to the company's financial position.

But the amount of information shown **on the face of** the balance sheet (on the main financial statement itself) is usually somewhat limited. Keep in mind that it is really a brief summary of the main items and for much of the detail you will have to turn to the **notes to the accounts**. For example, the main classes of asset are listed, but for the details of the liabilities you will have to turn to the notes.

In practice, most companies listed on the stock exchange will produce two balance sheets in their report and accounts. One will be headed **consolidated balance sheet** or **group balance sheet**. The other will be headed **balance sheet** or **company balance sheet**. The difference is important.

Most listed companies are in fact groups of companies: sometimes dozens or even hundreds of them. There is a top company which is usually called the **parent company** or **holding company**. SimpleCo plc is the top company in our example. This top company in turn owns and controls other companies, known as **subsidiary companies** or **subsidiaries**, by owning all or a majority of their voting shares. It may be that there is a separate subsidiary company for each of the main activities undertaken by the business. The top company and its subsidiaries, viewed as a whole, are often referred to as the **group**.

We have used the terms 'company' and 'group' pretty much interchangeably, except where we want to stress the difference between the two. This is, in fact, common practice in writing about companies. But for 'company' you should really read 'group of companies' except where the context suggests otherwise.

A consolidated balance sheet or group balance sheet lumps together the assets and liabilities of all the companies in the group, treating the group as if it were a single entity. The figures that are headed simply 'balance sheet' or 'company balance sheet' deal with the assets or liabilities of the top company. It is the consolidated balance sheet that is most informative for most purposes and is the one that you should look at. Some companies, instead of producing two balance sheets, simply show the figures for the company and the group in separately headed columns on a single sheet. This can be confusing. Always make sure that it is the consolidated figures that you are looking at.

The most common format for the balance sheet of a listed company starts by listing the **assets** (what the company owns) then progressively knocks off the **liabilities** (what the company owes). Once all the liabilities have been deducted you are left with a figure for **net assets**: the assets less all liabilities. This is the value in accounting terms of the owners' interest in the company: the **shareholders' interest**.

The bottom part of the balance sheet then shows the make-up of the shareholders' interest in the company: what was financed by the issue of shares, what was financed from profits retained in the business, and so on.

Sticking to our earlier format, we have shown the assets of the company in light grey and the liabilities that must be deducted in red. They are, of course, unlikely to appear like this in a real-life company balance sheet.

Assets and liabilities are both classified according to whether they are long-term or short-term. **Fixed assets** are long-term assets and **current assets** are short-term assets. **Creditors (due within one year)** are short-term liabilities, **creditors (due after one year)** are longer-term liabilities. We will look in more detail at what this means on page 13.

Balance sheet

What the company owns and what it owes

Fixed assets are the long-term assets of the business. In this case they are all **tangible assets** such as plant, machinery and properties: items you could touch. Some companies will also have **intangible assets**, which would include items like goodwill, trade names, patents and copyrights. These can have a value and are clearly an asset of the business but cannot be touched like physical assets.

Current assets are the short-term assets like stocks of materials and cash in the bank which are constantly changing in the course of business.

Creditors (due within one year) are the short-term liabilities of the business, including short-term bank loans. They are sometimes called **current liabilities**.

Deduct the short-term liabilities from the short-term assets and you end up with **net current assets** of £9m. If short-term liabilities exceeded short-term assets, you would have **net current liabilities** here.

This gives the result of putting together the fixed assets and the net current assets. It therefore shows the assets of the business after the short-term liabilities have been deducted.

Creditors (due after one year) are the longer-term liabilities of the business. They would include loans and parts of loans where repayment is not due for more than a year but also very long-term liabilities such as forms of borrowing that are not repayable for 20 years or more.

Finally, we have the **net assets** of the business: what is left after all the liabilities have been allowed for. But remember that this is simply an accounting figure. It does not tell you what the company will be worth in the stock market or, necessarily, what would be left in practice if the company's assets were sold and its debts repaid.

SimpleCo plc

CONSOLIDATED BALANCE SHEET AS AT 31 DECEMBER

	£m	£m
FIXED ASSETS		
TANGIBLE ASSETS		30
CURRENT ASSETS		
STOCKS	11	
DEBTORS	18	
CASH AT BANK	5	
	34	
CREDITORS (DUE WITHIN ONE YEAR)	25	
NET CURRENT ASSETS/(LIABILITIES)		9
TOTAL ASSETS LESS CURRENT LIABILITIES		39
CREDITORS (DUE AFTER ONE YEAR)		10
NET ASSETS		29
CAPITAL AND RESERVES		
CALLED UP SHARE CAPITAL	10	
SHARE PREMIUM ACCOUNT	4	
PROFIT AND LOSS ACCOUNT	15	
SHAREHOLDERS' FUNDS		29

Long-term assets of the business

We now need to look at the main balance sheet items in a little more detail. Take assets first.

Accounts in Britain are produced mainly on an **historical cost** basis. What that means is that most assets are shown in the accounts at what they cost originally, less allowances for wear and tear (**depreciation**). This is not always the case. Some assets, particularly **properties**, are sometimes revalued and the new values are taken into the accounts. But in our example even the properties (**land and buildings**) are shown at cost.

The notes to the balance sheet will give more detail about the company's assets. We have shown on page 15, in simplified form, what the note on tangible assets might show.

SimpleCo's tangible fixed assets comprise **plant and equipment** and **land and buildings** (or **properties**). Some companies lease the properties they operate from; others own them. Our company owns at least some of the properties it occupies.

At the start of the note we see that the plant and equipment that SimpleCo owned at the beginning of the year had originally cost £31m. Its land and buildings had originally cost £15m. During the year the company spent £5m on additional plant and equipment but did not buy any further properties. So, at the year-end, it had plant and equipment that had cost £36m originally and properties that had cost £15m.

Next comes **depreciation**. All plant and equipment eventually wears out and has to be replaced. Each year a company makes a deduction from its profits to recognise that it has used up part of the life of its plant and equipment during the year. This **depreciation charge** is one of the costs that is deducted before arriving at operating profit and would be shown as a note to the profit and loss account. It does not represent a physical transfer of money – merely an item that needs to be allowed for to give a true picture of profits.

In our example, the accumulated amount of depreciation that SimpleCo had provided in earlier years was £13m in respect of plant and equipment and £4m in respect of land and buildings. These were the amounts it had set aside from profits, year by year, to reflect the wearing-out of these items.

In the latest year it has provided from the year's profits further depreciation of £3m on plant and equipment and £1m on land and buildings. This takes the total of accumulated depreciation up to £16m and £5m respectively.

Deduct these amounts from the original cost of the assets and you find that plant and machinery have a **net book value** or **depreciated value** of £20m and the corresponding figure for land and buildings is £10m. Together, these figures of £20m and £10m make up the £30m figure shown for tangible assets on the face of the balance sheet.

The size of the depreciation charge is normally calculated so as to write off the cost of assets over their useful lives. But the depreciated values shown in the accounts are not necessarily the second-hand value of the assets if they were to be sold. This could be affected by a lot of different factors.

Cost	Plant and equipment £m	Land and buildings £m
At start of year	31	15
Additions	5	0
At end of year	36	15
Depreciation		
At start of year	13	4
Provided during year	3	1
At end of year	16	5
Net book value at end of year	20	10

SimpleCo plc

CONSOLIDATED BALANCE SHEET AS AT 31 DECEMBER

	£m	£m
FIXED ASSETS		
TANGIBLE ASSETS		30
CURRENT ASSETS		
STOCKS	11	
DEBTORS	18	
CASH AT BANK	5	
	34	
CREDITORS (DUE WITHIN ONE YEAR)	25	
NET CURRENT ASSETS/(LIABILITIES)		9
TOTAL ASSETS LESS CURRENT LIABILITIES		39
CREDITORS (DUE AFTER ONE YEAR)		10
NET ASSETS		29
CAPITAL AND RESERVES		
CALLED UP SHARE CAPITAL	10	
SHARE PREMIUM ACCOUNT	4	
PROFIT AND LOSS ACCOUNT	15	
SHAREHOLDERS' FUNDS		29

Assets that are on the move

The **current assets** of a company are the assets which are constantly on the move. **Stocks** of raw materials are being used up in the manufacturing process and replaced as necessary. Stocks of finished goods are being sold to customers and replaced with new production. **Cash** is going out as payments have to be made and cash is coming in as payments are received. And the money owing to the company, shown under the heading of **debtors**, is constantly changing as further goods are supplied to customers and payment is received for goods that had been supplied earlier.

In the notes to the accounts the stocks that SimpleCo holds are probably broken down between stocks of **raw materials**, **work-in-progress** (goods in the process of manufacture at the balance sheet date) and stocks of **finished goods**. In the case of our gnome-maker this might equate to stocks of raw plastic, gnomes which have been moulded and await painting, and the finished gnomes, packaged and awaiting dispatch.

Stocks are normally shown in the accounts at 'the lower of cost or realisable value'. This means they are normally shown at what they cost. But if their value should have fallen – perhaps because the materials or components involved have become obsolescent – then the figures in the accounts will need to be written down to what they are worth.

Stock control is an important part of managing the finances of a company. The company needs to be sure that manufacturing is not brought to a halt by a shortage of essential raw materials and components. On the other hand, the company has to use its cash to buy stocks, and holding an unnecessarily high level of stocks will soak up cash and lead to higher interest costs.

All else being equal, if the company's business expands (as measured by turnover) you might expect the amount of stocks it holds to need to increase, which will soak up cash. You might be a bit worried if stocks had increased but turnover had remained static or fallen. It could suggest that the company was manufacturing more than it could sell.

Debtors also need tight control. Customers do not normally pay for products immediately. Typically, they might have something between one and three months to pay for goods they have received. This is known as **trade credit**. Effectively, SimpleCo is making an interest-free loan to its customers. The figure for debtors shows the amounts that are owing to the company.

A well-run company will chase customers for amounts owing that are overdue, but some customers are slow payers. And some may never pay, because they go bust. In this case our company has probably lost the money owing to it. This will need to be written off as a **bad debt**. Remember that excessive debtors are a burden on the finances of our company – it has not yet got the money in from customers, but it has had to shell out cash for the raw materials and other costs involved in making the product.

Cash at the bank is the money the company has available for its immediate needs. All else being equal, it will probably reduce if the company needs to spend money on increasing the level of stocks it holds or on providing larger volumes of trade credit (i.e., running up a bigger figure for debtors). The consequences of allowing stocks and debtors to get out of control are illustrated on pages 84–5. Money that is tied up in the day-to-day running of the business, and shown under current assets, is often referred to as **working capital**, though different people define this term in slightly different ways.

Stocks

	£m
Raw materials and consumables	5
Work in progress	3
Finished goods	3
	11

The figure for **debtors** will probably be broken down in the notes between **trade debtors** (customers who have not yet paid) and other types of debtor. Remember that trade debtors really represent interest-free loans that SimpleCo is making to its customers and they tie up its cash resources.

The cash that the company has available may be broken down between **cash at bank and in hand** – which is the most immediately available – and **short-term bank deposits** which is available at relatively short notice.

SimpleCo plc

CONSOLIDATED BALANCE SHEET AS AT 31 DECEMBER

	£m	£m
FIXED ASSETS		
TANGIBLE ASSETS		30
CURRENT ASSETS		
STOCKS	11	
DEBTORS	18	
CASH AT BANK	5	
	34	
CREDITORS (DUE WITHIN ONE YEAR)	25	
NET CURRENT ASSETS/(LIABILITIES)		9
TOTAL ASSETS LESS CURRENT LIABILITIES		39
CREDITORS (DUE AFTER ONE YEAR)		10
NET ASSETS		29
CAPITAL AND RESERVES		
CALLED UP SHARE CAPITAL	10	
SHARE PREMIUM ACCOUNT	4	
PROFIT AND LOSS ACCOUNT	15	
SHAREHOLDERS' FUNDS		29

Short-term debts of the business

Creditors (due within one year) are the counterpart of current assets. They comprise the company's short-term liabilities and are, indeed, sometimes known as **current liabilities**. If you deduct these short-term liabilities from the company's short-term assets, you get a figure for **net current assets** (or for **net current liabilities** if the short-term liabilities are larger than the short-term assets, as they sometimes are).

The net current assets figure gives a measure of the amount of money tied up in the day-to-day running of the business. Some people adopt this as their definition of **working capital**.

Irritatingly, while the detail of current assets is probably shown on the face of the balance sheet, you may have to turn to the notes to the accounts to get the detail of the short-term liabilities. On page 19 we show the main items which are likely to be included under this heading.

Trade creditors are the counterpart of trade debtors. They represent money the company owes to people who have supplied it with goods and services but who have not yet been paid. With our gnome-maker, the suppliers of the raw plastics that it uses would almost certainly figure among its trade creditors. So this is money that the company will have to shell out in the fairly near future.

Younger and smaller companies often find it difficult to persuade suppliers to let them have goods on credit and may have to pay promptly. More established concerns will expect their suppliers to give them a period of free credit before they have to pay. Effectively, this is an interest-free loan from the suppliers and it puts off the day when the company will have to dip into its cash to pay.

A company which has been earning profits will normally have to pay **corporation tax** (company tax) on these profits. At any given time it will probably have an outstanding liability for tax that has not yet been paid but which will become due in the fairly near future. This liability for corporation tax is therefore also a short-term liability.

The **proposed dividend** is also cash that will have to be disbursed fairly soon. Most companies pay their dividend in two parts. The **interim dividend** is paid in the course of the year and the **final dividend** is normally proposed by the directors after the year's results are known but is not paid until shareholders have voted to approve it at the **annual general meeting (agm)**. Thus, at the point at which the accounts are drawn up it is money which the company expects to pay out in the near future.

Finally, the short-term liabilities include any borrowed money which might have to be repaid within a year. We have shown only a **bank overdraft**, which is theoretically repayable on demand. But many other kinds of short-term borrowing might be shown here, including more esoteric items such as commercial paper or bills of exchange.

Some companies satisfy all their borrowing needs with short-term loans of one kind or another, which will appear under **creditors due within one year**. But it is not always the safest policy, as short-term loans can often be withdrawn more easily than the longer-term forms of loan which will appear under **creditors (due after one year)**. You will see later that SimpleCo has longer-term borrowings as well as an overdraft.

Creditors due within one year

	£m
Trade creditors	14
Corporation tax	2
Proposed dividend	2
Bank overdraft	7
	25

Bank overdraft. Any form of borrowing that is repayable within one year will be shown here. An overdraft is technically repayable on demand, even though in practice it may run much longer, so it has to be shown as a short-term borrowing. Also shown here will be any instalments of longer-term loans which are repayable within a year.

Proposed dividend. This will probably be the cost of the final dividend for the year just ended. It has been proposed but will not be paid until it has been approved by the shareholders at the annual general meeting, so at this point it is a liability.

Corporation tax. This is the tax liability the company has incurred on its profits which will need to be paid within a fairly short time.

Trade creditors. These are the counterpart of trade debtors. They are amounts that the company owes, but has not yet paid, for goods and services it has received. Since trade credit does not normally bear interest, this is in the nature of a free loan to the company from its suppliers. Some companies deliberately delay settling their bills for this reason.

SimpleCo plc

CONSOLIDATED BALANCE SHEET AS AT 31 DECEMBER

	£m	£m
FIXED ASSETS		
TANGIBLE ASSETS		30
CURRENT ASSETS		
STOCKS	11	
DEBTORS	18	
CASH AT BANK	5	
	34	
CREDITORS (DUE WITHIN ONE YEAR)	25	
NET CURRENT ASSETS/(LIABILITIES)		9
TOTAL ASSETS LESS CURRENT LIABILITIES		39
CREDITORS (DUE AFTER ONE YEAR)		10
NET ASSETS		29
CAPITAL AND RESERVES		
CALLED UP SHARE CAPITAL	10	
SHARE PREMIUM ACCOUNT	4	
PROFIT AND LOSS ACCOUNT	15	
SHAREHOLDERS' FUNDS		29

Looking at the long-term debt

A company's longer-term borrowings will appear under the heading **creditors (due after one year)**. This heading could also include other forms of long-term liability such as trade credit which does not have to be settled within a year. But for simplicity we have assumed that SimpleCo's long-term liabilities are confined to various kinds of loan.

The 9% Debenture stock 2009 represents money the company has borrowed, like the overdraft we saw appearing under short-term liabilities. But it is a different kind of borrowing, because it is a **security**.

In essence, the company has borrowed money by issuing a **bond**. Investors were prepared to lend money to the company – in this case £7m in total – and in return they received a piece of paper from the company, acknowledging the debt, agreeing to pay 9% a year interest and agreeing to repay the money in the year 2009: its **redemption** or **maturity** date.

Investors who decide they want their money back before the year 2009 can simply sell their pieces of paper to other investors, who then acquire the right to receive the annual interest and the repayment of the money in 2009.

From SimpleCo's point of view, the advantage of borrowing money by issuing a **fixed-interest bond** is that it knows it will have the use of the money until the year 2009 and knows what it will have to pay in interest charges – provided it pays the interest on time and keeps to the other terms of the bond.

Term loans are not a security like a bond. They have more in common with an overdraft. SimpleCo borrows money, probably from a bank or a group of banks, and repays this money to the same banks when due. But with the term loan, unlike the overdraft, the company borrows the money for a specific period; perhaps five years. Provided it keeps to the terms of the loan, it knows that it will have the use of the money for this time.

Sometimes a term loan will be repayable in full at the end of the term – five years in our example – and sometimes it will be repayable in instalments during its life. If any of the instalments were due within a year, they would need to be shown under short-term creditors rather than long-term ones. And when the loan comes to within a year of its repayment date, the whole loan will need to be shown under short-term liabilities.

Traditionally, most companies try to match their assets and liabilities. They are more likely to take out long-term loans which will appear under **creditors (due after one year)** to buy long-term assets such as plant, equipment and buildings which will appear under the heading of **fixed assets**. They are more likely to use short-term loans like bank overdrafts to buy short-term assets like stocks of materials, where the amounts they need may fluctuate at different times of year. But this is by no means a universal rule. Some companies use only short-term loans, others use only long-term loans and some use no borrowed money at all.

SimpleCo plc

CONSOLIDATED BALANCE SHEET AS AT 31 DECEMBER

	£m	£m
FIXED ASSETS		
TANGIBLE ASSETS		30
CURRENT ASSETS		
STOCKS	11	
DEBTORS	18	
CASH AT BANK	5	
	34	
CREDITORS (DUE WITHIN ONE YEAR)	25	
NET CURRENT ASSETS/(LIABILITIES)		9
TOTAL ASSETS LESS CURRENT LIABILITIES		39
CREDITORS (DUE AFTER ONE YEAR)		10
NET ASSETS		29
CAPITAL AND RESERVES		
CALLED UP SHARE CAPITAL	10	
SHARE PREMIUM ACCOUNT	4	
PROFIT AND LOSS ACCOUNT	15	
SHAREHOLDERS' FUNDS		29

Creditors due after one year

	£m
9% Debenture stock 2009	7
Term loans	3
	10

Creditors due after one year does not mean that these liabilities are payable in exactly a year. They fall due any time from a year onwards. They include bonds with a life of more than a year (the **debenture** here is a form of bond) and bank or other loans that are not repayable within a year. For more detail on these loans you need to go to the notes to the accounts. Important points to look out for are when they are repayable and whether they carry a fixed or floating rate of interest. The debenture shown here is a bond that carries a fixed interest rate or **coupon** of 9% and is repayable in the year 2009. Without looking at the notes we do not know whether the **term loans** are at a fixed or floating rate. The difference is important because it tells you whether or not the company would be badly hit if short-term interest rates rose sharply. But be a bit careful. The company may have borrowed floating rate money but purchased a **cap** or other form of **hedging instrument** to insure itself against a rise in interest rates.

Assets that remain for the shareholders

The ordinary shareholders are the owners of a company – in legal jargon they are described as the **members** of the company. After a company has allowed for all its debts and other liabilities to outside parties, what remains belongs to the shareholders. But this needs a little explanation.

Take our example company. Its **assets** – what it owns – comprise £30m of **fixed assets** and £34m of **current assets**. Its **total assets** (or **gross assets**) are therefore £64m. Against this, it 'owes' £25m in the form of short-term debts and other liabilities – shown as **creditors (due within one year)** – and £10m in the form of long-term debts: **creditors (due after one year)**. Its **total liabilities** are therefore £35m.

If you deduct this £35m of liabilities from the total assets of £64m, you are left with a figure of £29m. This £29m is the **value for accounting purposes** of the shareholders' interest in the company, since it is what is left when all the liabilities have been allowed for. It is the **net asset value** of the company ('net', because the liabilities have been deducted from the 'gross' assets).

But you have to be careful about what this figure really means. In theory, SimpleCo could decide to wind itself up, sell all its assets, pay all its liabilities out of the proceeds and have £29m left to distribute among its shareholders.

In practice, the sums would be very unlikely to work out quite like this. The £30m figure for fixed assets reflects what these assets originally cost, reduced for wear and tear. It does not necessarily tell you what they would fetch if you tried to sell them today. Similarly with the stocks shown under current assets. This is why we say that £29m is the **value for accounting purposes** of the shareholders' interest in the company. It is not necessarily what the shareholders would get if the company were wound up.

Nor does the £29m necessarily tell you anything about the **market value** of the shareholders' investment in the company. The value of companies on the stock market is determined by what investors are prepared to pay for their shares. And this, in turn, is usually determined by the profits the company earns or is capable of earning.

The breakdown of the shareholders' money in the business – the **shareholders' funds** – does, however, tell us something about where this money came from. We will look at this point in more detail on page 24. But there is one point to get clear at the outset, which sometimes poses problems. The fact that there is £29m of shareholders' money in the business does not mean that SimpleCo includes among its assets a £29m pot labelled 'belongs to shareholders'.

All the money a company raises, whether by borrowing it, by selling shares to shareholders or by ploughing back part of its profits, goes into a common pot. All of this money can be used for any of the purposes of the company: buying plant or machinery, buying stocks, paying the employees. Some is probably held ready for use in a bank account. The money in the company – or the assets bought with it – does not belong to a particular party, regardless of where it came from in the first place.

However, money that has been borrowed must normally be repaid. So people who are owed money by the company (the company's **creditors**) will have a prior claim on its assets as a whole. If the company is wound up and its assets are sold, the creditors get their money back before shareholders receive anything. Some creditors may also have their loans **secured** on specific assets of the company, its properties, for example. In this case they have the first claim on the proceeds of selling the properties.

Net assets are what is left after deducting from the company's **assets** everything that it owes or knows that it will have to pay (in other words, its **liabilities**). With companies like investment trusts or property companies, which own assets that can readily be valued or sold, the net asset figure is important and may be the main factor determining the share price. With other types of company, net assets are usually less important. First, the net asset value is purely an accounting figure and does not necessarily tell you what would be left if the company sold its assets and repaid its debts. Second, most types of company are valued on the stock market by reference to the profits they are capable of earning rather than the assets that they own.

When you have deducted from its assets everything that a company owes, what remains is the accounting value of the shareholders' interest in the company. This is broken down under different headings to show the origin of the shareholders' money used in the business. Some was provided by the sale of shares or the use of shares to buy other businesses. Some came from the profits of earlier years that were ploughed back into the business rather than being distributed by way of dividends. The breakdown will be examined in more detail on the next sheet. The total value of the shareholders' interest in the company is usually referred to as **shareholders' funds**.

SimpleCo plc

CONSOLIDATED BALANCE SHEET AS AT 31 DECEMBER

	£m	£m
FIXED ASSETS		
TANGIBLE ASSETS		30
CURRENT ASSETS		
STOCKS	11	
DEBTORS	18	
CASH AT BANK	5	
	34	
CREDITORS (DUE WITHIN ONE YEAR)	25	
NET CURRENT ASSETS/(LIABILITIES)		9
TOTAL ASSETS LESS CURRENT LIABILITIES		39
CREDITORS (DUE AFTER ONE YEAR)		10
NET ASSETS		29
CAPITAL AND RESERVES		
CALLED UP SHARE CAPITAL	10	
SHARE PREMIUM ACCOUNT	4	
PROFIT AND LOSS ACCOUNT	15	
SHAREHOLDERS' FUNDS		29

Where the shareholders' money came from

The heading **shareholders' funds** in the balance sheet provides an historical record of the origin of the shareholders' money employed in the business.

When a company is formed, the founding owners **subscribe** for shares – probably at their **face value**. The money from the sale of these shares goes into the company's coffers. Subsequently, the company may raise further money by creating and issuing additional shares for cash. It may also create additional shares which are used as a 'currency' to buy other businesses or assets, rather than being issued for cash.

After a company has been going for some time, and if it has been successful, its shares are likely to become worth considerably more than their **face value (par value** or **nominal value)**. From this point on, the face value is largely irrelevant to shareholders, though it retains a significance for certain legal and accounting reasons.

If the company's shares are by this time listed on the stock market, their precise value at any one time will be determined by the interplay of buyers and sellers in the market. And the price that buyers are prepared to pay will be determined largely by the profit-earning potential of the company, and hence its ability to pay dividends and expand its business.

At this stage, if the company decides to raise further cash by creating and selling additional shares, it will almost certainly sell them at a price related to their market value. The price is therefore likely to be well above nominal value.

This explanation is necessary to illustrate how the shareholders' money in a company is accounted for. In the example on page 25 the total shareholders' money in the business for accounting purposes is £29m. These are the **shareholders' funds**. But this £29m is broken down under three categories (there could in practice be more).

The **called up share capital** is the nominal or face value of the shares that SimpleCo has issued.

Companies may choose what face value they like for their shares, but we have assumed a face value of 50p per share. Therefore every £1 of nominal capital shown here represents two 50p shares. Since there is £10m of nominal capital, SimpleCo has 20m 50p shares in issue (in America companies do not necessarily need a par value for their shares, which makes life a lot simpler!).

Every additional share SimpleCo might create and sell would therefore add 50p to the called-up share capital. But what if each share is sold at a much higher price than this, say 400p? How is the extra 350p **premium** over the 50p nominal value accounted for?

The answer is that it appears in a special form of reserve called the **share premium account**. A 50p share sold at 400p would therefore add 50p to called up capital and 350p to the share premium account. In our example this share premium account stands at £4m. SimpleCo has therefore, over its life, issued shares to a total value of £14m at the time. Of this, £10m represents the face value of the shares issued and the £4m represents the premium over this face value.

The third item of shareholders' funds is the **profit and loss account reserve**. This is where the company keeps a cumulative record of the profits it has ploughed back into the business year after year. We have seen that a company will normally distribute part of its profits to shareholders by way of dividend but that the remaining profits still belong to shareholders even though they are kept in the company and put to work to finance its future growth. This reserve will, of course, be reduced by any losses that the company makes.

The balance sheet therefore shows that, of the £29m of shareholders' money used in the SimpleCo business, £14m came from the issue of shares and £15m was provided by the profits ploughed back into the business over the years.

Called up share capital is the amount of share capital in issue at the year-end. It is not the same thing as **authorised share capital** which is the maximum amount the company can issue under its **Memorandum and Articles of Association** (effectively, the company's constitution). The notes will give details of authorised capital.

Note that share capital is shown as a money amount; this is the nominal amount of capital in issue. But each £1 of nominal capital might be divided into four shares of 25p each, ten shares of 10p each or (as we are assuming in the case of SimpleCo) two shares of 50p each. You may need to look at the notes to find the number of shares in issue.

The company may also have more than one class of share capital in issue. We have assumed in this simplified example that there is only one class of ordinary shares. But the company might also have **preference shares**, which are part of its share capital but not part of its *equity* **share capital** (see page 49).

When a company issues shares at a price above their **nominal** or **face value**, it has to account for the **premium** over face value. Thus, if a company issued 50p shares at 400p, each share issued would add 50p to called up share capital and 350p to **share premium account**. Because it arises from the issue of capital, special restrictions apply to the uses to which the share premium account may be put.

The profit and loss account reserve is where the company accounts for profits it has ploughed back into the business in previous years. Though this money was not distributed to shareholders as dividends, it counts as part of the shareholders' money in the business or **shareholders' funds**.

SimpleCo plc

**CONSOLIDATED BALANCE SHEET AS AT
31 DECEMBER**

	£m	£m
FIXED ASSETS		
TANGIBLE ASSETS		30
CURRENT ASSETS		
STOCKS	11	
DEBTORS	18	
CASH AT BANK	5	
	34	
CREDITORS (DUE WITHIN ONE YEAR)	25	
NET CURRENT ASSETS/(LIABILITIES)		9
TOTAL ASSETS LESS CURRENT LIABILITIES		39
CREDITORS (DUE AFTER ONE YEAR)		10
NET ASSETS		29
CAPITAL AND RESERVES		
CALLED UP SHARE CAPITAL	10	
SHARE PREMIUM ACCOUNT	4	
PROFIT AND LOSS ACCOUNT	15	
SHAREHOLDERS' FUNDS		29

How to calculate gearing

Why does it matter where the money came from to run the business? In practice it is vital to know how much **borrowed money** the company is using, and how this relates to the amount of **shareholders' (owners') money** employed.

Borrowed money can be very useful, if not essential. Used properly, it can allow the company to increase the return for ordinary shareholders ('**gear up** the returns on the equity' – see pages 76–7). But it also brings dangers.

Almost all borrowed money has to be repaid at some point. Moreover, **interest** will have to be paid on it at regular intervals. If the borrower does not keep to the terms of the loan – fails to pay the interest or to make the **capital repayments** when due – the lender can usually demand that the loan be repaid immediately. All too often this means that the business collapses.

Money provided by the owners in return for shares in the business does not normally carry this risk. The company will usually expect (and be expected) to pay a **dividend** on its share capital. But if it hits trouble and is unable to pay a dividend, shareholders are very unlikely to try to close the company down. Nor can they normally require repayment of the money they have put into the business in return for ordinary shares.

This is why **ordinary share capital** (or **equity capital**) is sometimes referred to as **permanent capital**. It is also known as **risk capital**, emphasising that the investor in ordinary shares is sharing in the risks and rewards of the business. If ordinary shareholders want their money back, this usually involves finding somebody else to buy the shares. Stock markets exist at least partly to bring such buyers and sellers together.

Many companies go bust as a result of using too much borrowed money in relation to the shareholders' money in the business. In good times when profits are high and the company is generating a lot of cash, it may have no problem in paying the large interest charges on its borrowings. But if trade turns down, things may look very different. As profits and cash flow fall, the company has more and more difficulty meeting its interest charges and may eventually be forced to give up the ghost.

For this reason lenders will, in any case, be reluctant to lend too much in relation to the shareholders' money in the business. **Gearing** is the term for this relationship between borrowed money and shareholders' money (Americans use the word **leverage** to mean the same thing). The gearing is one of the first things that a banker or investment analyst will look for in a company's accounts.

To calculate the gearing you add up all the **borrowed money** the company is using (which will be shown in short-term creditors and long-term creditors). This is then expressed as a percentage of the **shareholders' money** in the business (see opposite). Often the sum is performed using borrowed money less any cash held, in which case the result would be expressed as **net gearing** (see page 27).

Note that for this purpose money owed to **trade creditors** does not count as a borrowing. This is because interest is not normally paid on trade credit. On the other hand, where companies **lease** their assets under finance leases rather than owning them outright, the payment obligations under the lease will be included in borrowings.

SimpleCo plc

CONSOLIDATED BALANCE SHEET AS AT 31 DECEMBER

	£m	£m
FIXED ASSETS		
TANGIBLE ASSETS		30
CURRENT ASSETS		
STOCKS	11	
DEBTORS	18	
CASH AT BANK	5	
	34	
CREDITORS (DUE WITHIN ONE YEAR)	25	
NET CURRENT ASSETS/(LIABILITIES)		9
TOTAL ASSETS LESS CURRENT LIABILITIES		39
CREDITORS (DUE AFTER ONE YEAR)		10
NET ASSETS		29
CAPITAL AND RESERVES		
CALLED UP SHARE CAPITAL	10	
SHARE PREMIUM ACCOUNT	4	
PROFIT AND LOSS ACCOUNT	15	
SHAREHOLDERS' FUNDS		29

Total borrowings

Short-term

	£m
Bank overdraft (see page 19)	7

Long-term

	£m
9% Debenture stock 2009	7
Term loans (see page 21)	3
	17

Gearing ratios

The relationship between borrowed money and shareholders' money in a business – the **gearing** – is a vital ratio. It is usually expressed as **borrowings as a percentage of shareholders' funds**. In this case the £17m of **gross borrowings** are equivalent to 59% of the shareholders' funds of £29m. Sometimes the ratio is worked out instead on **net borrowings**, which in this case would be £12m: the £17m of gross borrowings less the company's **cash** of £5m. These net borrowings of £12m would be equivalent to 41.4% of the £29m figure for **shareholders' funds**.

Working out the assets per share

The value of a company – in the stock market or elsewhere – usually depends mainly on the profits that the company earns or is thought capable of earning. In the long run the profits determine the size of **dividend** the company is capable of paying. Increasing profits usually mean increasing dividends and – all else being equal – a rise in the value of the shares.

On the other hand, there are some types of company where the share price may be determined mainly by the value of the assets that the company owns. This is likely to be the case where the company's main business is owning assets in which there is a ready market and which can therefore be valued pretty easily and turned into cash if desired.

Investment trust companies (**investment trusts**) are one example. The main business for most of them is owning shares in other companies that are traded on a stock market, which can therefore be easily priced.

Property investment companies are another example. They own office, shop or factory and warehouse buildings which they hold as a long-term investment for the rents they produce from the tenants. There is a reasonably active market in such investment properties in Britain, which means that they can be reasonably accurately valued by a surveyor.

Other companies do not make a specific business of owning shares or properties, but happen to own large quantities – of properties, usually – in the course of their trade. Retail groups which own the stores that they operate from are one example.

Such readily valued assets can add to a company's attractions and may influence its share price. Investment analysts therefore frequently calculate a company's **net asset value per share**. This gives a figure for the amount of assets backing each share in issue.

This calculation involves deducting all the company's liabilities from the value of its assets to arrive at a figure for the **net assets** attributable to shareholders. Assuming that the company has only ordinary shares in issue, these net assets are then divided by the number of shares to give the **asset backing** for each share.

The calculation is easy in the case of SimpleCo. However, there are sometimes adjustments to make. If the company's fixed assets include some **intangible assets** – items like goodwill, patent rights or the like – these are normally stripped out of the net asset figure before performing the calculation. Strictly, therefore, analysts are normally calculating the **net tangible assets per share**.

On the other hand, some of the company's assets might be worth more than the figures at which they appear in the accounts (**stand in the books**). This could be the case if the company's properties stand in the books at cost but would have a **market value** considerably higher. The difference between the **book value** and the **market value** could be added into the net assets to give a more realistic picture of the true value of the assets backing the shares.

The price of shares in the market is sometimes described as 'standing at a **premium to assets**' (standing above the net asset value) or 'standing at a **discount to assets**' (standing below the asset value).

SimpleCo plc

CONSOLIDATED BALANCE SHEET AS AT 31 DECEMBER

	£m	£m
FIXED ASSETS		
TANGIBLE ASSETS		30
CURRENT ASSETS		
STOCKS	11	
DEBTORS	18	
CASH AT BANK	5	
	34	
CREDITORS (DUE WITHIN ONE YEAR)	25	
NET CURRENT ASSETS/(LIABILITIES)		9
TOTAL ASSETS LESS CURRENT LIABILITIES		39
CREDITORS (DUE AFTER ONE YEAR)		10
NET ASSETS		29
CAPITAL AND RESERVES		
CALLED UP SHARE CAPITAL	10	(20m shares)
SHARE PREMIUM ACCOUNT	4	
PROFIT AND LOSS ACCOUNT	15	
SHAREHOLDERS' FUNDS		29

Net asset value per share (NAV)

Though, for most types of company, assets are not the main determinant of the share price, **the asset backing** for each share in issue is still frequently calculated. The result is referred to as **net asset value per share** or **NAV**.

In our example there are 20m ordinary shares in issue (£10m of capital in 50p shares). Divide the £29m of net assets by the 20m issued shares and you have an asset backing of 145p per share. So 145p is the NAV.

Strictly, the figure should be referred to as the net *tangible* **asset value per share**. If the company has **intangible assets** in its balance sheet such as **goodwill**, the intangible items would usually be deducted from net assets before arriving at the NAV. SimpleCo does not have any such intangible assets.

Relating the accounts items to the share price

The information disclosed in a company's accounts clearly has an important bearing on the value of the shares in the company. The investment world uses a number of ratios to express the relationship between accounts items and the market price of the shares.

The most commonly quoted ratios are the **dividend yield** or simply **yield** and the **price-earnings ratio** or **PE ratio**. These two items will normally be quoted next to share prices in newspapers.

Investors clearly want to know what return they will be getting on their money when they buy a share at the market price, and this is where the dividend yield comes in. The basic sum is simple. If you pay 500p for a share that pays a dividend of 15p, you simply express the dividend as a percentage of the price you pay. In this case the answer is 3% (see opposite). But there are some caveats.

First, the yield tells you only what percentage return on your money you will get by way of annual income from the share: the **income return**. In practice, investors will hope that their **total return** or **overall return** will be higher than this, because they also hope to make capital gains as the share rises in value.

Second, the quoted yield figure will be based on the last dividends the company paid or the dividends it has forecast for the current year. The next dividend that the investor receives could be higher than the figure on which the yield calculation is based. It could also be lower if the company hits problems, or in the worst cases there might be no dividend at all.

The yield may help to show how the stock market rates a company's shares. As a general rule, a **low dividend yield** indicates a fast-growing company and a **high dividend yield** indicates a slower-growing concern. The reason is logical. Investors are prepared to pay a high price for a share and accept a low yield at the outset if they think that dividends (and therefore the return on their money) will be increasing rapidly in the future. It is also often the case that young and fast-growing companies pay fairly small dividends because they want to retain as much money as possible in the business to finance its expansion.

The **price-earnings ratio** also tells you something about the way investors rate a company. Essentially, it shows what price investors are prepared to pay for the shares in the stock market in relation to the profits the company earns for each share. You calculate the PE ratio by dividing the earnings per share into the share price (see page 31).

A **high PE ratio** tends to indicate a fast-growing company and a **low PE ratio** a less dynamic concern. Again, this is logical. In relation to the profit a company earns today, you would be prepared to pay a reasonably high price for the shares if you thought those profits would increase very rapidly in the future. You would expect to pay considerably less in relation to today's profits if you did not expect much by way of future profits growth or if you thought the company was unduly risky.

Note that commentators often talk of a **prospective dividend yield** or a **prospective PE ratio**. This is where they base the relevant calculation on forecast or estimated dividends or earnings for a future year, rather than the published figures for the past year. Note, too, that the word **multiple** (of earnings) is often used as a synonym for PE ratio.

STOCK MARKET RATIOS

The main investment ratios relate the company's share price to information from its accounts: notably, earnings and dividends.

The **price–earnings ratio** or **PE ratio** relates the share price to the net profit earned for one share (the **earnings per share** figure). It is thus a measure of the value that investors put on a company's earnings.

The **yield** or **dividend yield** relates the share price to the dividend that the company pays. It thus shows the income return – as a percentage of the money spent – to an investor who buys the shares at the market price (though of course the size of the dividend could change in the future).

DIVIDEND YIELD CALCULATION

$$\frac{\text{DIVIDEND PER SHARE} \times 100}{\text{MARKET PRICE}} = \text{YIELD}$$

Or, in the example,

$$\frac{15p \times 100}{500} = 3\%$$

PRICE–EARNINGS RATIO CALCULATION

$$\frac{\text{MARKET PRICE}}{\text{EARNINGS PER SHARE}} = \text{PE RATIO}$$

Or, in the example,

$$\frac{500}{35} = 14.3$$

SimpleCo plc

SUMMARY FINANCIAL INFORMATION FOR YEAR TO 31 DECEMBER

NUMBER OF ORDINARY SHARES IN ISSUE	20m shares of 50p
SHARE PRICE	500p
	£m
NET PROFIT AFTER TAX	7
less DIVIDENDS	3
RETAINED PROFIT	4
Earnings per share	35p
Dividend per share	15p

Cash in and cash out – how does it balance?

When investment analysts or journalists comment on a company's performance, it's usually the profit figures that they quote. When bankers look at a business to see if it's a suitable candidate for a loan, they are probably more interested in the company's **cash flow** projections than in its profit forecasts – at least in the short term.

Though profit and cash flow are related, they are not necessarily the same thing. If you sell for £1,000 something that cost you £700 to make, you have made a profit of £300. But if the customer has six weeks to pay, you don't receive the cash till later. So you might chalk up a profit of £300 on the day that you make the sale, but the cash will not show up in your accounts for six weeks. Indeed, you have to be careful. You have had to use your own cash to pay the costs of producing what you sell. But you don't get cash back until the customers pay. If they take too long to pay, or if you sell too many products on generous credit terms, you could find yourself running out of cash. And businesses risk going bust when they run out of cash.

The movements of cash into and out of a company are therefore a vital guide to its financial health and viability. If there is more cash flowing out of a company than into it, you would want to know why. And this is why companies are nowadays required to produce a **cash flow statement** as well as a profit and loss account.

To understand what the cash flow statement sets out to show, think of the cash flows into and out of a typical company. It receives cash as a result of its day-to-day operations, from the goods and services that it sells. However, as we've seen, there may be a delay before this cash comes in. Until they have paid, customers are **debtors** of the company. If the company is increasing its sales, the customers that owe it money at any given time are probably increasing too. The figure for debtors will rise. This absorbs the company's cash resources.

At the same time, the company is having to pay its running costs. Cash is going out to pay for raw materials, to pay wages, rent, rates, energy costs, and all the other expenses of running the business. The company probably does not have to pay all of these costs immediately. Its suppliers of raw materials may themselves be prepared to wait six weeks for payment. In the meantime, they will be **trade creditors** of the company. They are, in effect, making short-term interest-free loans to the company, just as the company is effectively making interest-free loans to its trade debtors. If the figure for trade creditors increases, this increases the company's cash resources.

So we would look first at whether the company is generating enough cash from its operations to cover its running costs (including the interest it has to pay, the tax due to the government and its dividend to shareholders).

But there are other calls on a company's cash. It is probably spending money on additional plant and equipment. Is it generating enough cash from its operations to cover this, or will the cash have to be found elsewhere? It may, of course, also bring in some cash from selling plant or equipment that is now surplus to requirements.

Our company may also be shelling out cash to buy other businesses, if it is intending to expand by acquisition. Or, again, it could be raising cash by selling subsidiary businesses which are no longer thought to fit into the group.

Spending on plant and equipment or on buying other businesses are **capital items** and are a bit different from spending on day-to-day operations, which qualify as **revenue items**. So we would probably look first at whether the company is generating enough cash from its day-to-day operations to cover its day-to-day costs (the revenue side of the account). Then we would see

These items show the cash flowing in or out over the year as a result of the company's day-to-day operations. These are all items relating to the company's **revenue** and include interest paid during the year (less interest received) and corporation tax paid to the government. Many people would include the cost of the dividends paid during the year under this heading, though it is actually shown lower down.

These two headings show the movements of cash related to **capital items**. First comes the cash spent on buying new plant and equipment (fixed assets) less any cash received from the sale of assets. Next is shown the cash spent on buying other businesses or raised from the sale of businesses – we've assumed there were no such transactions during the year.

Here we can see whether the company generated more cash than it spent, or whether the outflow exceeded the inflow.

Finally, the statement shows the effect of **financing operations** during the year: repayment of loans, raising new loans, issuing further shares for cash etc., and whether the cash held by the company increased or decreased over the period.

SimpleCo plc

CONSOLIDATED CASH FLOW STATEMENT FOR THE YEAR ENDED 31 DECEMBER

	£m
CASH FLOW FROM OPERATING ACTIVITIES	14.00
RETURNS ON INVESTMENTS AND SERVICING OF FINANCE	−1.50
TAXATION	−2.40
CAPITAL EXPENDITURE AND FINANCIAL INVESTMENT	−5.00
ACQUISITIONS AND DISPOSALS	0.00
EQUITY DIVIDENDS PAID	−2.80
CASH INFLOW (OUTFLOW) BEFORE USE OF LIQUID RESOURCES AND FINANCING	2.30
MANAGEMENT OF LIQUID RESOURCES	0.00
FINANCING	−3.00
INCREASE/(DECREASE) IN CASH FOR THE PERIOD	−0.70

whether the total cash it is generating covers its capital costs as well. The result will be a **cash inflow** or a **cash outflow**.

So far, so good. Then we have to look at the company's purely financial operations. Has it repaid loans during the year, which would represent a cash outflow? (SimpleCo has, in fact, done this.) Or has it issued new shares for cash, or raised additional loans, either of which would bring fresh cash into the company? Finally, we can combine the effect of **financing operations** with the cash inflow or outflow that we calculated earlier to see whether the amount of cash held by the company has risen or fallen.

Arriving at the cash flows

Though cash flow is not the same thing as profit, the profit figures are the starting point for calculating the cash flow. You can see opposite some of the adjustments that have to be made to derive the cash flow from the profit figures. In a real set of company accounts, much of this information is given in the notes rather than in the cash flow statement itself.

Start with the operating profit or loss. This is not the same thing as the cash flowing into or out of the company. For a start, **depreciation** is deducted before arriving at operating profit in the profit and loss account, but depreciation is only an **accounting item**. It does not represent a real flow of cash out of the company. So we add the depreciation provision back in.

Next, look at the figures for **stocks** and **trade debtors**. If the company has increased its holdings of stocks over the year, or if it is lending more money to customers than a year earlier, these increases represent additional cash that the company has had to spend. So we have to deduct them from the cash flowing into the company. On the other hand, an increase in **trade creditors** represents additional amounts that suppliers are lending to the company, so this is an extra flow of cash into the company. After allowing for these items, the cash flow into the company from its operating activities comes out £2m higher than its operating profit.

The next heading includes the **interest paid** by the company, less any **interest received**. Note that this is the interest actually paid during the year, not the interest liability that the company incurred during the year. In the profit and loss account the reference will be to 'interest payable', because the company has to show the liability to pay interest that built up during the year, even if the interest did not have to be paid until after the year-end. In the cash flow statement it shows the interest payments it actually made. The same principle applies with any interest received.

Taxation will cover UK **corporation tax** and any foreign company taxes paid during the year. Again, the crucial word is 'paid'. It is not the same thing as the tax liability incurred during the year, which the profit and loss account shows.

Dividends, again, are the payments actually made to shareholders during the year. A final dividend is usually paid after the year-end and the cost of the interim and final is shown in the profit and loss account. But what you probably see in the cash flow statement is the **final dividend** for the previous year and the **interim dividend** for the year in question, as these were the amounts actually shelled out during the year.

We can see that SimpleCo had more than enough cash coming in to cover its interest payment, tax payments and dividends, which together absorb only £6.7m of the £14m operating cash flow, leaving £7.3m spare.

Next we look at a different kind of expenditure, **capital expenditure**. This is divided into two parts: cash used to buy additional **fixed assets** (plant, machinery, property, etc.) and cash laid out to buy **additional businesses**. In the two cases we can deduct, respectively, any cash received from the sale of assets or of businesses owned by the company. In our example SimpleCo has spent £5m of cash in buying further fixed assets but has received nothing from the sale of assets. But it has not made any acquisitions or disposals of other companies during the year. One point to note: when companies buy other businesses they will also be buying any cash that these businesses own, and this cash inflow will need to be accounted for in the cash flow statement.

Our example thus shows a healthy cash flow picture. Not only has SimpleCo generated more than enough cash to cover its cash outflows on day-to-day operations (interest costs, tax, the cost of the dividend, etc.) but it also generated enough cash to cover its capital expenditure. Though it has

Operating profit	12.00
Depreciation charges	
Increase in stocks	−2.00
Increase in debtors	−3.00
Increase in creditors	
	―――
Net cash inflow (outflow) from operating activities	

Interest received	
Interest paid	−2.00
	―――
Net cash inflow (outflow)	−1.50

Purchase of tangible fixed assets	−5.00
Sale of plant and machinery	0.00
	―――
Net cash inflow (outflow)	−5.00

Purchase of subsidiary undertaking	0.00
Sale of business	0.00
	―――
Net cash inflow (outflow)	0.00

SimpleCo plc

CONSOLIDATED CASH FLOW STATEMENT FOR THE YEAR ENDED 31 DECEMBER

	£m
CASH FLOW FROM OPERATING ACTIVITIES	14.00
RETURNS ON INVESTMENTS AND SERVICING OF FINANCE	−1.50
TAXATION	−2.40
CAPITAL EXPENDITURE AND FINANCIAL INVESTMENT	−5.00
ACQUISITIONS AND DISPOSALS	0.00
EQUITY DIVIDENDS PAID	−2.80
	―――
CASH INFLOW (OUTFLOW) BEFORE USE OF LIQUID RESOURCES AND FINANCING	2.30
MANAGEMENT OF LIQUID RESOURCES	0.00
FINANCING	−3.00
	―――
INCREASE/(DECREASE) IN CASH FOR THE PERIOD	−0.70
	―――

run down its cash holdings slightly by repaying a £3m loan, it had no need to bring in fresh cash from outside.

This is not always the case. Fast-growing companies frequently use up cash more rapidly than they can generate it. In this case they may need to bring in additional cash by raising fresh loans or issuing additional shares for cash to cover heavy spending on fixed assets or the cost of buying additional businesses. There is not necessarily anything wrong with this, though you might want to check that the company was not over-extending itself by going on a spending splurge (look particularly at the gearing ratio – see pages 26–7).

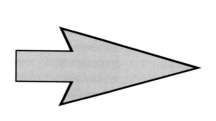

Cash generated internally and cash from outside

SimpleCo was generating a healthy cash flow from its operations, its spending on fixed assets was relatively modest and it did not acquire any additional businesses during the year. The result is that it had £2.3m more cash flowing in than flowing out over the year, before taking account of its repayment of a £3m loan. This will not always be the case. A company may have more cash flowing out than flowing in, and in this case we have to see where the additional cash came from to cover the shortfall.

The important heading here is **financing**. This is where you will see a record of any new cash raised from outside the company as a result of new borrowings or the issue of new shares for cash. You will also see whether any existing cash was used to repay earlier loans.

SimpleCo has not raised any additional cash from outside over the year. Instead, it has applied £3m of its existing cash to repaying some of its borrowings. Since this exceeds its net cash inflow of £2.3m for the year, the result is a slight reduction in its holdings of cash. The company has run down the cash it holds at the bank, which will be shown in the balance sheet under the **current assets** heading, by £700,000.

The heading we have not so far explained is **management of liquid resources**. This can be a bit confusing and as it is something of a technicality we have not included any transactions under this heading. What it amounts to is this. As well as cash at the bank a company may have other **liquid** resources (liquid really means something that can be liquidated – turned into cash – fairly readily). Perhaps it has holdings of government bonds. These bonds are not cash; they cannot themselves be used to pay bills but they can be sold in the stock market and thus turned into cash in a day or so. Technically, therefore, a company that uses part of its cash to buy bonds is reducing its cash resources, whereas it is increasing its cash resources if it sells bonds that it owns to turn them into cash. This heading records transactions of this kind, where something that is fairly close to cash is turned into cash, or vice versa.

Much of the information in the cash flow statement can, in fact, be deduced from the profit and loss account and from movements in balance sheet items over the year. But the cash flow statement cuts down on the detective work and helps to answer one very important question: is the company generating or can it obtain enough cash to sustain its activities and to cover the cost of any expansion that it has in mind?

This is one of the first things that any serious student of company accounts will look at. Remember that companies go bust when they run out of cash. So start with the balance sheet. From the current assets heading you can see that SimpleCo still had £5m of cash in the bank after the £3m loan repayment that the cash flow statement discloses. You also know from the cash flow statement that the company had a healthy cash inflow from its operations last year and you might assume, unless there is evidence to the contrary, that it will again generate a healthy amount of cash in the current year. On the face of it SimpleCo should have or be able to generate enough cash for its needs, given its current scale of operations. But note that if the company suffered a severe profits setback, this would almost certainly cut the amount of cash flowing in as well.

Now suppose that SimpleCo is planning a much bigger **capital investment programme** (i.e. much more spending on **fixed assets**) in the current year. Perhaps it is equipping a new factory. Would it have the cash to cover the cost? You might deduce that the company would not want to use up all the cash that it has – companies need a 'float' of cash to be able to operate – and that the cash that it will generate during the year will probably not be quite enough to cover the planned expenditure. This

Cash inflow (outflow) **before use of liquid resources and financing**

This shows whether the company was generating more cash than it was spending, after taking account of its capital transactions as well as its revenue transactions, but before allowing for fresh cash raised (or cash paid back) during the year.

Management of liquid resources

Cash withdrawn from 7-day deposit	0.00
Purchase of gov't securities	0.00
Net cash inflow (outflow)	0.00

Financing

Issue of ordinary share capital	0.00
Debt due within a year	
Increase in short-term borrowings	0.00
Repayment of secured loan	−3.00
Net cash inflow (outflow)	−3.00

Increase/(decrease) **in cash for the period**

This shows the effect on the amount of cash that the company holds of all the cash flows into and out of the company over the year. You may check it against the balance sheet, where you can see how much cash the company held at the end of its latest year and in the previous year.

SimpleCo plc

CONSOLIDATED CASH FLOW STATEMENT FOR THE YEAR ENDED 31 DECEMBER

	£m
CASH FLOW FROM OPERATING ACTIVITIES	14.00
RETURNS ON INVESTMENTS AND SERVICING OF FINANCE	−1.50
TAXATION	−2.40
CAPITAL EXPENDITURE AND FINANCIAL INVESTMENT	−5.00
ACQUISITIONS AND DISPOSALS	0.00
EQUITY DIVIDENDS PAID	−2.80
CASH INFLOW (OUTFLOW) BEFORE USE OF LIQUID RESOURCES AND FINANCING	2.30
MANAGEMENT OF LIQUID RESOURCES	0.00
FINANCING	−3.00
INCREASE/(DECREASE) IN CASH FOR THE PERIOD	−0.70

probably means that it will need to raise additional cash from outside. Can it do so?

We saw earlier that the company's net borrowings were equal to 41% of shareholders' funds. This is not excessive and the company might be able to borrow a bit more money if it wanted to. But the chances are that it might not want to see its **gearing** (see pages 26–7) rise much higher, so it might decide instead to raise the additional cash it will need by creating and selling new ordinary shares (we will look at the mechanism later). This would increase the amount of **shareholders' money** in the business, thereby reducing the gearing, and would make it easier to raise further loans in the future if the company needs to. Since SimpleCo is earning good profits and has a good reason for needing the additional cash, it should not have much trouble in persuading investors to buy the new shares.

'It was the danger and excitement that attracted me to accountancy.'

Cartoon reproduced by permission of The Spectator.

Some additional features that crop up in practice

We looked earlier at the main elements of the **profit and loss account** and **balance sheet**. Now we need to look at some additional complications that crop up in practice, and for this purpose we've created a set of accounts for a slightly more complex company. It is called ComplexCo, though in reality it is still relatively simple. You'll see that the main items remain pretty much unchanged, but there are some new features. Take the profit and loss account first.

Most 'companies', as we saw at the outset, are not in fact single companies but groups of companies under a common parent: the **parent company** or **holding company**. We saw also that **group accounts** or **consolidated accounts** lump together the profits and losses and assets and liabilities of the companies in the group as if it were a single entity.

But so far we have assumed that the parent company owns the whole of any other companies in the group (the **subsidiaries**) by owning all of the share capital of each of them. This may be the case, but it is not necessarily so.

It may be that the parent company has some subsidiaries where it owns more than 50% of the voting share capital – thereby controlling them – but does not own the whole share capital. There are other shareholders – **outside shareholders** or **minority shareholders** – who have a smaller stake in the particular subsidiary.

Suppose ComplexCo bought a controlling interest in another company (perhaps a family business – we'll call it FamilyCo) some time back. It acquired, say, 80% of the FamilyCo share capital. However, the founding family wanted to retain a direct stake in the business they managed and they hung on to the other 20% of FamilyCo's shares.

This means that 20% of the profits or losses of FamilyCo belong to these minority shareholders, not to ComplexCo's shareholders. However, ComplexCo accounts for FamilyCo by including the whole of FamilyCo's profits in its group accounts. Then, at the post-tax level, it makes a deduction for the proportion of the net profits of FamilyCo that belong to the minority shareholders, not to its own shareholders. If FamilyCo had made a loss, the parent would have included the whole of the losses in its group accounts, then added back at the net level the proportion of these losses that was attributable to the minority shareholders. We have assumed in the example that FamilyCo made profits after tax of £500,000, of which £100,000 (20%) was therefore attributable to the minority shareholders.

Only after deducting the profits (or adding back the losses) that are attributable to minority shareholders can ComplexCo arrive at the profits that are attributable to its own shareholders. Its **earnings per share** are calculated on these attributable profits – its **equity earnings** – after the minority interests have been allowed for, and not on the immediate post-tax profit figure. In the example there is also one other deduction – for preference dividends – that has to be made before arriving at equity earnings and we will examine this on pages 48–9.

Now take the case of another business where ComplexCo has a significant stake – say, between 20% and 50% – but which it does not control as it controls FamilyCo. It also exerts some management influence on this company, which we'll call JointCo. Suppose, for simplicity, that our company set up the JointCo business in association with a couple of partners. It took 30% of the JointCo shares and the two partners took 30% and 40% respectively. Perhaps the JointCo was set up to supply components to all three owners.

Our company does not control JointCo, which is not therefore a subsidiary but an **associated company** or **related company**, and the accounting is different.

Associated undertakings are often referred to as **associated companies** or **associates**. They are not subsidiaries, but are businesses in which our company has a significant share stake – probably between 20% and 50% – and over which it exerts some management influence.

ComplexCo includes in the profit and loss account its share of the profits (or losses) of these associates. If the associates made profits of £10m and our company had a 30% stake, it would take credit for 30% of these profits, or £3m.

Note that ComplexCo probably does not have the use of all of this £3m profit. All it receives in cash is any dividends paid by the associated company, which are probably only a proportion of the associate's profits.

ComplexCo does not necessarily own 100% of the share capital of all its subsidiaries. It might control a company – we've called it FamilyCo – where it owns 80% of the share capital and other shareholders – known as **minority shareholders** or **outside shareholders** – have the remaining 20%.

These minority shareholders are therefore entitled to 20% of the profits of FamilyCo. ComplexCo includes the whole of the profit of this subsidiary in its group accounts, then makes a deduction after tax – described as **minority interests** – for the proportion of FamilyCo's profit that is attributable to the minority shareholders.

Our company works out the profit attributable to its own shareholders – in this case £8.2m – after minority interests and preference dividends (see pages 48–9) have been allowed for.

ComplexCo plc

CONSOLIDATED PROFIT AND LOSS ACCOUNT FOR THE YEAR ENDED 31 DECEMBER

	£m
TURNOVER	100.00
OPERATING PROFIT	12.00
add SHARE OF PROFITS OF ASSOCIATED UNDERTAKINGS	3.00
PROFIT BEFORE INTEREST	15.00
less INTEREST PAYABLE	2.00
PROFIT BEFORE TAX	13.00
less CORPORATION TAX	4.30
NET PROFIT AFTER TAX	8.70
less MINORITY INTERESTS	0.10
less PREFERENCE DIVIDEND	0.40
EQUITY EARNINGS	8.20
less ORDINARY DIVIDENDS	3.00
RETAINED PROFIT	5.20
Earnings per share	41p
Dividends per share	15p

(20m 50p ordinary shares and 5m £1 preference shares in issue)

Our company simply includes 30% (its pro-portionate share) of the profits or losses of JointCo in its own profit and loss account. If JointCo made £10m in total, our company takes £3m into its own accounts, which is the figure we've assumed.

Note that it probably does not have the benefit of the whole of this £3m in cash. All it will receive is the dividend that JointCo pays to its three owners, which is probably much smaller (if, indeed, JointCo pays a dividend at all). The **cash flow statement**, with its associated notes, will make this clear. It is another case where reported profit may be very different from cash received.

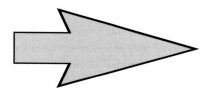

Allowing for preference shares

So far, when we have talked about shares, it has been **ordinary shares** that we have referred to (also known as **equity**). But many companies have more than one class of share capital, and it is common to find **preference shares** as well as ordinary shares.

As their name suggests, preference shares normally have preference for payment of dividends. This means that ordinary shareholders will not receive any dividend until the preference dividends have been paid. Preference shares normally pay a fixed dividend, rather like a fixed-interest bond. An 8% preference share with a face value of £1 would thus pay a dividend of 8p.

This is no guarantee that the preference dividend will be paid. If the company is making losses and short of cash, it may have to suspend payment of preference as well as ordinary dividends (**pass the dividend**). However, if the preference shares are also **cumulative** (which is denoted by the abbreviation **cum** in their description), the owners of the preference shares are entitled to receive any arrears of dividend when the company resumes payments – again, before the ordinary shareholders get anything.

If a company is **wound up (liquidated)**, the preference shareholders are normally entitled to receive back the nominal value of their shares (usually £1) plus any **arrears of dividend**, before anything is paid to the ordinary shareholders. However, a company which is compulsorily liquidated is normally in such a bad way that there is nothing left for preference or ordinary shareholders. Those who are owed money by the company – the **creditors** – have a prior right to any money available.

Preference shares are also sometimes **redeemable**, denoted by the abbreviation **red** in their title. This means that they will be repaid by the company at some future point, rather like a bond.

All of this shows that preference shares are rather safer for the investor than ordinary shares. Their disadvantage is that they do not normally participate in the growth of the company. A preference share which pays a fixed dividend of 8p pays 8p each year, however much the company's profits increase.

However, you will occasionally come across variants of the preference share. There are **participating preference shares** which probably pay a fixed basic dividend plus an amount on top that is geared to the dividend paid on the ordinary shares.

More commonly, there are also **convertible preference shares**. These give the shareholder the right to convert the preference shares into ordinary shares at a fixed price in the future. Thus, they offer the greater security of a preference share initially, with the possibility of sharing in the growth in value of the ordinary shares in the future.

Remember the principle. Whatever profits the company earns belong to the **ordinary shareholders** only after all other claims on these profits have been met. If the company has preference shares as well as ordinary ones, the **preference dividends** will be one of these claims.

ComplexCo plc

CONSOLIDATED PROFIT AND LOSS ACCOUNT FOR THE YEAR ENDED 31 DECEMBER

	£m
TURNOVER	100.00
OPERATING PROFIT	
add SHARE OF PROFITS OF	
ASSOCIATED UNDERTAKINGS	3.00
PROFIT BEFORE INTEREST	15.00
less INTEREST PAYABLE	2.00
PROFIT BEFORE TAX	13.00
less CORPORATION TAX	4.30
NET PROFIT AFTER TAX	8.70
less MINORITY INTERESTS	0.10
less PREFERENCE DIVIDEND	0.40
EQUITY EARNINGS	8.20
less ORDINARY DIVIDENDS	3.00
RETAINED PROFIT	5.20
Earnings per share	41p
Dividends per share	15p

(20m 50p shares in issue)

Preference shares are part of share capital, but not part of **ordinary** (or **equity**) **share capital**. They normally pay a fixed dividend, which does not rise with the improving fortunes of the company. Thus, they have quite a lot in common with a fixed-interest loan.

However, because preference shares are share capital, the dividends have to be paid out of profits that have borne corporation tax. **Preference dividends** are therefore shown as a deduction from net profits before arriving at the profits (or **earnings**) attributable to the ordinary shares.

In this example there are both minority interests and preference dividends to deduct before arriving at the equity earnings of £8.2m on which the earnings per share are calculated.

A closer look at associates

We saw earlier how ComplexCo accounted in its profit and loss account for its share of the profits of its **associated company**, in which it has a 30% share stake. Here we see how the same associate is dealt with in the **group balance sheet**.

Much the same principle applies. ComplexCo takes credit for its proportionate share of the net assets of the associated company. In our example, the associated company has net assets of £30m and a 30% share therefore comes to £9m. ComplexCo includes this £9m as an investment under the heading of 'fixed assets'.

It is sometimes worth looking a little more closely at the associated companies. The **borrowings** of the associate do not appear on ComplexCo's balance sheet, but they may be substantial. Let us suppose that the associate has gross assets of £62m and total liabilities of £32m, which leave net assets of £30m. If we assume that most of these liabilities are borrowed money, it is clear that the associate is much more heavily borrowed than our own company.

This need not matter. ComplexCo is not necessarily responsible for the borrowings of the associate, or even for its proportionate share of these borrowings. On the other hand, if it had given **guarantees** for the borrowings of the associate, it could be called on to repay this money if the associate got into difficulties and was unable to do so. This could be a very onerous liability.

If ComplexCo had given guarantees for loans that the associate had raised, this should be stated in a note to the accounts which would probably be headed **contingent liabilities**.

Money borrowed by group companies that do not qualify as subsidiaries – like our associated company – does not appear in ComplexCo's consolidated balance sheet. It is sometimes referred to as **off balance sheet finance**.

In the past, off balance sheet financing techniques were extensively used, particularly by property development companies, to disguise the full extent of the debts of the business. Accounting rules have now been tightened up and it is now more difficult to disguise liabilities in this way. But wherever a company operates partly through joint ventures, associated companies or other forms of partnership, the detail deserves scrutiny. This was an important factor in the Enron collapse.

Another item in the balance sheet that we have not come across before is the **provision for liabilities and charges**. This is where the company recognises various liabilities that will arise in the future, though the exact amount or the timing is not always precisely known. For example, ComplexCo may have received tax relief (by way of **capital allowances**) on its purchases of plant and equipment. If these assets were to be sold, some of the tax relief might need to be repaid. The company may also have made certain promises to pay pensions in the future, which are not fully funded (in other words, the money to provide the pensions has not been set aside in a separate fund). This future liability is likely to be acknowledged here.

However, a company does not normally make provisions against potential liabilities which, though they exist, are thought unlikely to arise in practice. For example, if a company were to sell its land and buildings it would probably be liable for tax on the rise in their value. But if it has no intention of selling them it would not make a provision to cover this potential liability.

Associated companies

Where our company has **associates**, it includes its share of the net assets of the associated company or companies as **investments** under the general heading of **fixed assets**. An abbreviated balance sheet of the associated company might look like this:

	£m
TOTAL ASSETS	62
less TOTAL LIABILITIES	32
NET ASSETS	30

ComplexCo has a 30% stake in the associate, so it includes 30% of the associate's net assets of £30m in its own accounts. This means, however, that the liabilities of the associate do not appear in ComplexCo's group accounts and they may – as in this case – be large.

Provisions for liabilities and charges

Where a company knows that it has various liabilities that will crop up in the future, even though they are not yet firm debts, it will recognise them under this heading. The company may know that it will have to meet the cost of certain staff pensions which are not otherwise provided for. Or it may expect that it is going to have to repay some tax relief that it had received earlier. The notes to the accounts will give the detail.

ComplexCo plc
CONSOLIDATED BALANCE SHEET AS AT 31 DECEMBER

	£m	£m
FIXED ASSETS		
TANGIBLE ASSETS	30.00	
INVESTMENTS (ASSOCIATED COMPANY)	9.00	
		39.00
CURRENT ASSETS		
STOCKS	11.00	
DEBTORS	18.00	
CASH AT BANK	5.00	
	34.00	
CREDITORS (DUE WITHIN ONE YEAR)	25.00	
NET CURRENT ASSETS (LIABILITIES)		9.00
TOTAL ASSETS LESS CURRENT LIABILITIES		48.00
CREDITORS (DUE AFTER ONE YEAR)		
9% DEBENTURE STOCK 2009	7.00	
TERM LOANS	3.00	
		10.00
PROVISIONS FOR LIABILITIES AND CHARGES		3.00
NET ASSETS		35.00
CAPITAL AND RESERVES		
CALLED UP SHARE CAPITAL		
ORDINARY SHARES (50p)	10.00	
PREFERENCE SHARES (£1)	5.00	
SHARE PREMIUM ACCOUNT	4.00	
PROFIT AND LOSS ACCOUNT	15.00	
SHAREHOLDERS' FUNDS	34.00	
MINORITY INTERESTS	1.00	
CAPITAL EMPLOYED		35.00
Comprising		
EQUITY SHAREHOLDERS' FUNDS		29.00
NON-EQUITY SHAREHOLDERS' FUNDS		5.00
EQUITY MINORITY INTERESTS		1.00
		35.00

What belongs to the ordinary shareholders

We looked earlier at the vital distinction between the borrowed money and the shareholders' money used in a business. But the shareholders' money itself needs to be examined more closely because it may consist of different types. The broad distinction is between **equity funds** and **non-equity funds**.

Where a company has only one class of capital – **ordinary shares** that carry one vote each – there is no problem. These ordinary shares are equity. Their owners share fully in the risks and rewards of the business and the business belongs to them after all its liabilities have been allowed for.

Where there are **preference shares** in addition to ordinary shares, the position is more complex. The preference shares, as we saw earlier, are part of the **shareholders' funds** but not part of the **equity shareholders' funds**. This is because they are normally entitled to a fixed dividend, plus a fixed repayment at the end of the day. They do not share fully in the risks and rewards of the business.

Though preference shares are, in legal terms, share capital and completely different from a loan, for some purposes they are best regarded almost as if they were a loan. In particular, you need to deduct what is attributable to the preference shareholders before you can work out the value of the **ordinary** (or **equity**) **shareholders' interest** in the company.

In our example this is quite easy. We have assumed there are 5m preference shares with a face value of £1 each and that these shares are ultimately repayable at £1. Clearly, the amount of shareholders' money in the business which is not attributable to the equity shareholders is therefore £5m. Deduct this £5m from the £34m total for shareholders' funds and you are left with £29m attributable to the equity.

But it is not always quite as simple as this. The company might have 5m preference shares with a face value of £1 but where each preference share had the right to be repaid at £2 in certain circumstances. In this case £5m of the company's reserves would need to be attributed to the preference shares to recognise that their holders had a claim on it. This amount would not therefore be attributable to the ordinary shareholders. The equity shareholders' funds would therefore reduce to £24m.

It is for reasons such as this that a balance sheet nowadays has to show clearly what is attributable to the ordinary shareholders (the **equity funds**) and what is attributable elsewhere (the **non-equity funds**).

The balance sheet should also make clear whether any **minority** interests are equity or non-equity. In the case of our FamilyCo subsidiary, where the family founders kept 20% of the shares and our company has the remaining 80%, we've assumed that it is ordinary shares that we are talking about and these minority interests therefore fall within the equity category. But the minority interests are not, of course, part of the shareholders' funds of ComplexCo.

In practice there are a lot of different formats that companies use to distinguish between the equity and non-equity shareholders' funds used in the business. Don't be surprised if you come across examples where the information is presented in a slightly different way.

Equity and non-equity

Accounting standards require the **capital and reserves** of a company to be divided between **equity interests** and **non-equity interests**. In the example, ComplexCo has £5m of **preference shares**, which are part of the share capital but not part of the equity share capital and reserves.

Total shareholders' funds are therefore £34m, but £5m of this represents the preference share capital. Therefore the **ordinary (or equity) shareholders' funds** are only £29m.

To calculate the **net assets per ordinary share** you would divide this £29m figure by the 20m ordinary shares in issue. The result, expressed in pence, would be 145p (see pages 28–9).

Attributing the assets

In calculating **net assets**, the whole of the assets and liabilities of the subsidiary in which ComplexCo had only an 80% interest (we called it FamilyCo) have been included. But not all of these assets and liabilities belong to ComplexCo. The **minority shareholders** own 20% of FamilyCo.

This is dealt with as follows. The proportion of the net assets of FamilyCo that are attributable to the minority shareholders are shown as a separate item and are not included in the shareholders' funds of ComplexCo.

The £1m attributable to the outside shareholders is shown as **equity minority interests** since they own 20% of the **ordinary** shares of this subsidiary company.

ComplexCo plc

CONSOLIDATED BALANCE SHEET AS AT 31 DECEMBER

	£m	£m
FIXED ASSETS		
TANGIBLE ASSETS	30.00	
INVESTMENTS (ASSOCIATED COMPANY)	9.00	
		39.00
CURRENT ASSETS		
STOCKS	11.00	
DEBTORS	18.00	
CASH AT BANK	5.00	
	34.00	
CREDITORS (DUE WITHIN ONE YEAR)	25.00	
NET CURRENT ASSETS/(LIABILITIES)		9.00
TOTAL ASSETS LESS CURRENT LIABILITIES		48.00
CREDITORS (DUE AFTER ONE YEAR)		
9% DEBENTURE STOCK 2009	7.00	
TERM LOANS	3.00	
		10.00
PROVISION FOR LIABILITIES AND CHARGES		3.00
NET ASSETS		35.00
CAPITAL AND RESERVES		
CALLED UP SHARE CAPITAL		
ORDINARY SHARES (50p)	10.00	
PREFERENCE SHARES (£1)	5.00	
SHARE PREMIUM ACCOUNT	4.00	
PROFIT AND LOSS ACCOUNT	15.00	
SHAREHOLDERS' FUNDS		34.00
MINORITY INTERESTS		1.00
CAPITAL EMPLOYED		35.00
Comprising		
EQUITY SHAREHOLDERS' FUNDS		29.00
NON-EQUITY SHAREHOLDERS' FUNDS		5.00
EQUITY MINORITY INTERESTS		1.00
		35.00

When the shape of the group is changing…

Companies of a size to be listed on the stock market are, as we saw at the outset, generally groups of companies rather than single entities.

But companies are not static. From year to year they may acquire new businesses or shut down or sell existing ones. Sometimes this will involve buying or selling complete companies. Sometimes it will simply involve starting up or closing down a particular activity within a group company.

Thus, the constituents of a company may be constantly changing, sometimes in a significant way, sometimes only at the fringes. But these changes can make it very difficult to compare the financial results of one year with those of the next. To illustrate the point we have invented another company, ActiveCo, which has clearly been going in for some restructuring.

There is an allied problem. In the course of these changes, the group may make profits or incur losses that are not part of its normal on-going business. In its latest year, ActiveCo made a profit of £2m on the sale of a factory building that had become surplus to requirements. And it incurred a loss of £7m in disposing of an under-performing subsidiary company that had to be sold for less than had been invested in it.

Let us suppose for the moment that ActiveCo is a machine-tool maker. Selling factories is not part of its normal business. Nor is selling or buying subsidiary companies. These are both **capital transactions** rather than **revenue items**. Moreover, they are likely to be **one-off** or **exceptional** transactions. Our machine-tool maker will not be selling a surplus factory every year. Nor will it be disposing of an under-performing subsidiary.

Though the profits or losses on capital transactions such as these need to be shown in the profit and loss account, they may often obscure the company's profit-earning capability from its ongoing businesses. For this reason, **accounting standards** require a group's profits to be broken down in a number of different ways. They must identify separately the **one-off profits** or **losses** that cropped up during the year but which are regarded as **exceptional**. The profit and loss account must also distinguish between profits or losses from businesses that were **discontinued** during the year, from new businesses that were **acquired** during the year and from the **on-going constituents** of the group.

All of these separately identified items – profits from new businesses or businesses that have been sold, plus one-off profits or losses on the sale of assets or whole businesses – must be included in arriving at ActiveCo's pre-tax profits and its **official earnings** per share. On the other hand, the one-off exceptional items in particular will often distort the company's on-going profits trend, which is what most accounts users are primarily concerned with.

ActiveCo made a capital loss of £7m on the sale of its under-performing subsidiary. But we can also see that the business it disposed of contributed £10m to the group's turnover but made an operating loss of £1m prior to disposal. ActiveCo's operating profits would have been higher at £15m without this loss, and it will not recur next year now the business has gone.

We assume, since there is no separate heading for profits from businesses acquired during the year, that ActiveCo had made no acquisitions.

As well as the £7m exceptional loss on the sale of the business, there was the £2m exceptional profit on the sale of the surplus factory. So, on balance, the exceptional items reduced published profits by £5m.

Profit and loss account

When the shape of the group is changing...

In the left-hand column of figures, the year's results are shown before allowing for 'one-off' **exceptional items**. The exceptional items are then shown in the middle column and the right-hand column marries the exceptional items with the results of normal trading shown in the left-hand column. It is the figures in the right-hand column that show the 'official' profit outcome for the year.

Turnover and **profit** are broken down between the results of **continuing operations** and the results of operations that have been **discontinued** during the year. If ActiveCo had acquired new business during the year, the results from these **acquisitions** would also have needed to be separately identified.

ActiveCo plc

CONSOLIDATED PROFIT AND LOSS ACCOUNT FOR THE YEAR ENDED 31 DECEMBER

	Before exceptional items £m	Exceptional items £m	Total £m
TURNOVER			
CONTINING OPERATIONS	90.00		90.00
DISCONTINUED OPERATIONS	10.00		10.00
	100.00		100.00
OPERATING PROFIT			
CONTINUING OPERATIONS	13.00		13.00
DISCONTINUED OPERATIONS	−1.00		−1.00
	12.00		12.00
LOSS ON SALE OF BUSINESS		−7.00	−7.00
PROFIT ON SALE OF PROPERTY		2.00	2.00
add SHARE OF PROFITS OF ASSOCIATED UNDERTAKINGS	3.00		3.00
PROFIT BEFORE INTEREST	15.00	−5.00	10.00
less INTEREST PAYABLE	2.00		2.00
PROFIT BEFORE TAX	13.00	−5.00	8.00
less CORPORATION TAX			2.60
NET PROFIT AFTER TAX			5.40
less MINORITY INTERESTS			0.10
less PREFERENCE DIVIDEND			0.40
EQUITY EARNINGS			4.90
less EQUITY DIVIDENDS PAID			3.00
RETAINED PROFIT			1.90

Dealing with one-off items

There are a number of different formats a company can use for its profit and loss account to identify the results of **acquisitions**, of **on-going businesses** and of **discontinued activities** and to highlight the **exceptional items**. We have chosen a format which shows, in the left-hand column, the results before taking into account the exceptional items. The next column shows these exceptional items. Then the right-hand column shows the results after taking into account the exceptional items. Sometimes the same information will be presented in a slightly different format.

It is the figures in the right-hand column that provide the figures for **profits** and **earnings** required by the relevant **accounting standard (FRS 3)**. Thus, ActiveCo has made profits of £8m before tax and the earnings available for ordinary shareholders are £4.9m.

However, these figures do not give a good picture of the group's **earning capacity** – and this is what most accounts users (and particularly stock market investors) are interested in.

Most companies therefore also produce an earnings figure based on profits before exceptional items. This is often calculated according to a formula advocated by the former **Institute of Investment Management and Research (IIMR)** which is now merged with another body to form the **Society of Investment Professionals**. It may be described as **IIMR earnings** or **headline earnings** or various other terms such as **sustainable earnings** (which is a bit misleading) or **normalised earnings**.

The **official earnings** figure based on profits after all exceptional items have been taken into account may be described as **FRS3 earnings** after the accounting standard that applies.

Companies that want to publish their own version of earnings – on an IIMR or any other basis – as well as the official FRS3 earnings figure must justify their reasons for doing so. Since the reason is normally obvious, the justification may be pretty cursory.

In the case of ActiveCo, earnings per share would have come out at 41p on an IIMR basis which excludes the exceptional items. Once the exceptional items are taken into account, the official FRS3 earnings are only 24.5p.

This is a big difference. Arguably the 41p IIMR earnings figure provides the best base for calculating the earnings the company is likely to produce in future years when there may be no exceptional items. It is likely to be the earnings figure used by newspapers and others in calculating **PE ratios** (see pages 30–1).

If we wanted to be clever, we should perhaps also adjust for the £1m loss made by the subsidiary business that has now been disposed of. This, too, will not recur next year. Such calculations are a bit more complex. The effect of the disposal of the subsidiary company will depend on how much money our company received from the sale, how it reinvested these proceeds and so on. Adding the £1m loss back into profits to calculate sustainable earnings would be a little simplistic, and for this reason earnings are not normally adjusted for items such as this, though investment analysts might attempt to calculate their effect on likely future profits.

Profit and loss account

Dealing with one-off items

The one-off **exceptional profits and losses** during the year are shown separately – in this case in a central column. They must, however, be included in the year's results, as shown under the heading of 'Total' in the right-hand column.

In a 'real life' profit and loss account, the figures shown here in the shaded area would probably not be provided, since the only 'official' figures are those in the right-hand column where **exceptional items** have been taken into account. We have included these figures to illustrate how the picture might have looked before the exceptional items, and to show the equity earnings on which an **IIMR earnings** figure (**headline earnings**) might have been calculated.

The 'official' **FRS3 earnings** figure of 24.5p per share is based on **equity earnings** of £4.9m, which reflects the year's one-off losses. The **IIMR earnings** figure of 41p is based on equity earnings of £8.2m, which would have been the probable figure had there been no **exceptional items** during the year.

In practice the figures are not always quite as simple as this, since the tax position on the one-off profits and losses may be complex.

ActiveCo plc

CONSOLIDATED PROFIT AND LOSS ACCOUNT FOR THE YEAR ENDED 31 DECEMBER

	Before exceptional items	Exceptional items	Total
	£m	£m	£m
TURNOVER			
CONTINUING OPERATIONS	90.00		90.00
DISCONTINUED OPERATIONS	10.00		10.00
	100.00		100.00
OPERATING PROFIT			
CONTINUING OPERATIONS	13.00		13.00
DISCONTINUED OPERATIONS	−1.00		−1.00
	12.00		12.00
LOSS ON SALE OF BUSINESS		7.00	7.00
PROFIT ON SALE OF PROPERTY		2.00	2.00
add SHARE OF PROFITS OF ASSOCIATED UNDERTAKINGS	3.00		3.00
PROFIT BEFORE INTEREST	15.00	−5.00	10.00
less INTEREST PAYABLE	2.00		2.00
PROFIT BEFORE TAX	13.00	−5.00	8.00
less CORPORATION TAX	4.30		2.60
NET PROFIT AFTER TAX	8.70		5.40
less MINORITY INTERESTS	0.10		0.10
less PREFERENCE DIVIDEND	0.40		0.40
EQUITY EARNINGS	8.20		4.90
less EQUITY DIVIDENDS PAID	3.00		3.00
RETAINED PROFIT	5.20		1.90
No. of ordinary shares in issue	20m		
No. of preference shares in issue	5m		
	Excluding exceptionals		FRS3 basis
Earnings per share	41p		24.5p

How convertible bonds work

To highlight another feature which crops up in many company accounts, we've reverted to a simplified profit and loss account to illustrate the principle. The feature in question is the **convertible bond** and we have called the example company ConvertibleCo plc.

Most conventional fixed-interest bonds are debt, plain and simple. They pay a fixed rate of interest throughout their life and are repaid (**redeemed**) at their face value at the end of this life.

Convertible bonds are different. They are still technically **debt** and therefore appear as a **liability** in the accounts. They almost certainly pay a **fixed rate of interest**. But the investor in convertible bonds has the right to convert them into ordinary shares if he wishes. The terms on which they may be converted are set when the convertible bonds are first issued.

For the investor, a convertible bond starts off offering the security traditionally associated with bonds. But later the investor can share in the company's growth by converting the bonds into shares. From the company's viewpoint, the interest rate on a convertible bond will probably be lower than on a **straight** (non-convertible) **fixed-interest bond**, so it saves in interest costs. The **interest** on the bond is also a deduction from profits before the tax charge is calculated – as with interest on other kinds of borrowing – so the company receives tax relief until the bond is converted into shares. The convertible bond will be included with other borrowings in calculating the company's **gearing**.

The **conversion terms** for the bond are normally pitched so that the **conversion price** is some way above the market price of the ordinary shares at the time it is issued. Suppose, therefore, that the market price of ConvertibleCo's shares was 220p when it issued the convertible bond some years back. The conversion terms were set at one ordinary share for every £2.50 of the bond's face

value. In other words, somebody who subscribed for the bond at its face value at the outset has the option to convert £2.50 of the bond into one share. This means that the share would effectively be costing him 250p, which was above the market price of the shares at the time of issue. Clearly, he will not convert the bond into shares until the share price in the market has risen above 250p.

In practice, he probably will not convert until the share price has risen a lot higher than 250p. This is because he probably gets a higher income yield on the bond than he would on the shares, so he may as well delay conversion as long as possible. Companies sometimes take powers to force convertible bondholders to convert when the share price has been above the conversion price for a reasonable period.

If the share price never rises above 250p in the life of the convertible bond, the bondholders will never convert. In this case the convertible bond is repaid by the company at its maturity date – perhaps fifteen years after it was issued. If the share price rises substantially, the price of the convertible bond in the stock market will also rise to reflect the increasingly valuable **conversion rights**.

Note that companies also sometimes issue **convertible preference shares** (sees pages 48–9) which may be converted into ordinary shares at the option of the shareholder. They work in much the same way as convertible bonds, but with two important differences. Since the convertible preference shares are **non-equity share capital**, they will be included under **capital and reserves** rather than under **liabilities**. They will not contribute to **borrowings** or to the company's **gearing** (as normally measured). But since they are share capital rather than debt, they pay a fixed dividend instead of interest, and the dividend has to be paid out of income that has borne corporation tax. In other words, there is no tax relief.

ConvertibleCo plc

CONSOLIDATED PROFIT AND LOSS ACCOUNT FOR THE YEAR ENDED 31 DECEMBER

	£m
TURNOVER	100
OPERATING PROFIT	12
less INTEREST PAYABLE	
BANK LOANS	1.2
CONVERTIBLE BOND	0.8
	2
PROFIT BEFORE TAX	10
less CORPORATION TAX	3
NET PROFIT AFTER TAX	7
less DIVIDENDS PAID	3
RETAINED PROFIT	4

Share price	500p
Earnings per share	35p
Dividends per share	15p

ConvertibleCo plc

CONSOLIDATED BALANCE SHEET AS AT 31 DECEMBER

	£m	£m
FIXED ASSETS		
TANGIBLE ASSETS		35
CURRENT ASSETS		
STOCKS	11	
DEBTORS	18	
CASH AT BANK	5	
	34	
CREDITORS (DUE WITHIN ONE YEAR)	25	
NET CURRENT ASSETS/ (LIABILITIES)		9
TOTAL ASSETS LESS CURRENT LIABILITIES		44
CREDITORS (DUE AFTER ONE YEAR)		
TERM LOANS	5	
8% CONVERTIBLE BOND	10	
		15
NET ASSETS		29
CAPITAL AND RESERVES		
CALLED UP SHARE CAPITAL	10	
SHARE PREMIUM ACCOUNT	4	
PROFIT AND LOSS ACCOUNT	15	
SHAREHOLDERS' FUNDS		29

Shares in issue   20m ordinary
Net asset value per share 145p

Doing the dilution sums with convertibles

You will sometimes come across the terms **fully diluted assets per share** or **fully diluted earnings** when dealing with the accounts of companies that have issued **convertible bonds** or **convertible preference shares**.

What **diluted** means in this context is as follows. When the convertible bond is converted into shares, the number of shares in issue will increase. From that point, whatever profits the company earns or whatever net assets it owns will need to be spread over a larger number of shares. This may have the effect of reducing (**diluting**) the **assets per share** and/or the **earnings per share**, though it will not always do so. It depends on the terms on which the convertible stock was issued initially and what has happened since.

When they come across a convertible stock, investment analysts and other accounts users will want to see how the company's figures are likely to be affected when it is converted. If profits will have to be spread over a much larger number of shares, it could affect the prospects for dividend increases in the future. So they make the assumption that the convertible is going to be converted immediately and, based on the current accounts, see what the accounts would look like after conversion.

We have done this with the balance sheet of ConvertibleCo on page 61 and will show the effect on the profit and loss account on pages 62–3.

When the convertible bond is fully converted into shares, it will no longer exist. In our example, its disappearance reduces the company's long-term liabilities – **creditors (due after one year)** – from £15m to £5m. The disappearance of this £10m liability has the effect of increasing the company's net assets from £29m to £39m.

Correspondingly, ConvertibleCo's **shareholders' funds** also increase by £10m. Remember that each £2.50 of the convertible bond converts into one new share of 50p nominal value. So conversion of the full £10m of convertible bond gives rise to the creation of 4m new shares or £2m of nominal capital. Therefore **ordinary share capital** rises from £10m to £12m. But the new shares are effectively issued at 250p each, so each new share created adds 50p to nominal capital and £2 to **share premium account**. This is why share premium account rises from £4m to £12m.

The disappearance of the convertible bond as a **liability** and the creation of £10m of additional **shareholders' funds** has a dramatic effect on ConvertibleCo's **gearing** (see pages 26–7). Including the £7m bank overdraft (which we have assumed features in **creditors due within one year**), gross borrowings were £22m before conversion and only £12m afterwards. **Gross gearing** falls from 76% to a much more comfortable 31%.

The new shares arising on conversion are effectively issued at 250p. This is above the pre-conversion **net asset value per share** of 145p. Therefore the conversion also, as it happens, has the effect of raising the company's net asset value – to 162p in our example. Therefore, this is a case where conversion enhances rather than dilutes the assets per share. We could therefore talk of a **fully diluted net asset value per share** of 162p and a **gross gearing** level of 31% **post-conversion**.

Balance sheet

Doing the dilution sums with convertibles

Once it is converted into shares, the **convertible bond** disappears as a liability from the balance sheet. This reduces **long-term creditors** from £15m to £5m.

The reduction of £10m in **long-term liabilities** leads to a corresponding increase of £10m in **net assets**.

The £10m of **convertible bond** converts into 4m new 50p shares, adding £2m to **issued capital**.

Each £2.50 of **convertible bond** that is converted into one share will add 50p to **issued capital** and £2 to **share premium account**.

By eliminating £10m of **borrowings** and substituting £10m of **capital and reserves**, the conversion of the **convertible bond** improves the company's **financial ratios** considerably. **Gearing** drops right back. And, as it happens, conversion also has the effect of increasing the **net asset value per share**, though this would not always be the case.

ConvertibleCo plc

CONSOLIDATED BALANCE SHEET AS AT 31 DECEMBER

	Before conversion		After conversion	
	£m	£m	£m	£m
FIXED ASSETS				
TANGIBLE ASSETS		35		35
CURRENT ASSETS				
STOCKS	11		11	
DEBTORS	18		18	
CASH AT BANK	5		5	
	34		34	
CREDITORS (DUE WITHIN ONE YEAR)	25		25	
NET CURRENT ASSETS/ (LIABILITIES)		9		9
TOTAL ASSETS LESS CURRENT LIABILITIES		44		44
CREDITORS (DUE AFTER ONE YEAR)				
TERM LOANS	5		5	
8% CONVERTIBLE BOND	10		0	
		15		5
NET ASSETS		29		39
CAPITAL AND RESERVES				
ORDINARY SHARE CAPITAL	10		12	
SHARE PREMIUM ACCOUNT	4		12	
PROFIT AND LOSS ACCOUNT	15		15	
SHAREHOLDERS' FUNDS		29		39

Ordinary shares of 50p in issue	20m	24m
Net asset value per share	145p	162p
Gross borrowings	£22m	£12m
Net borrowings	£17m	£7m
Gross gearing	76%	31%
Net gearing	59%	18%

How conversion affects earnings

Having looked at the balance sheet effects when a **convertible bond** converts, we now look at the effect on the **profit and loss account**. Remember that the company has £10m nominal of 8% convertible bond in issue and that each £2.50 of the bond converts into one 50p share.

The two sets of figures opposite show the company's income position before **conversion** and what the figures would look like if full conversion is assumed. We have made one further assumption: the convertible bond was originally issued, say, about six years back. The company has been very successful and by now its share price in the stock market has risen to 700p, well above the **conversion price** of 250p.

The first effect of conversion is that the £800,000 of annual **interest** payable on the convertible bond disappears. This has the effect of raising pre-tax profits from £10m to £10.8m. This results in a higher **corporation tax** charge. But the net profit after tax still rises from £6.7m to £7.24m.

However, these **earnings** have to be spread over a larger number of shares, since the conversion of the loan stock raises the number of 50p ordinary shares in issue from 20m to 24m (see pages 60–1). The result is a reduction in **earnings per share** from 33.5p to 30.15p. We would say that **fully diluted earnings** work out at 30.15p against **undiluted earnings** of 33.5p.

The **dividend** also has to be paid on a larger number of shares. Assuming that the dividend is held at the same level of 15p per share net, the cost of the dividend rises from £3m on 20m shares to £3.6m on the 24m shares after conversion. The result is a minor fall in the profits retained in the business and a reduction from 2.23 times to 2.01 times in **dividend cover**.

With a share price of 700p, the **PE ratio** is 20.90, based on the earnings before conversion. But if we allow for the reduction in **earnings per share** following conversion, the PE ratio at a share price of 700p would rise to 23.21. In other words, the shares look a bit more expensive if you allow for the effects of conversion than they did before.

In the example we have taken, the effects of conversion are not too damaging. The reduction in earnings per share is fairly small, though it could put some restraint on the rate of dividend growth. On the other hand, our conversion exercise is hypothetical. Investors in the convertible bonds might delay converting into shares for a few more years (if they are allowed to under the terms of the convertible bond). If earnings have grown further by the time conversion actually takes place, the effect of the **dilution** will be greater.

Many company directors persuade themselves that a convertible bond allows them effectively to make a deferred issue of new shares at a price above the market price at the time of issue. They tend to forget that, by the time conversion takes place, they may effectively be issuing shares at a price well below their market value. For fast-growing companies, convertible bonds are not always as cheap a source of finance as some people think.

The cost of the **interest** on the **convertible bond** disappears when it is converted into shares, which has the effect of increasing the **profit before tax**.

Though **net profits after tax** are higher following conversion, these **earnings** have to be spread over a larger number of shares. In our example, this results in a fall in **earnings per share**.

The same **dividend per share** costs more when it has to be paid on the larger number of shares resulting from conversion.

With the reduction in **interest charges** following conversion, **interest cover** improves (see pages 8–9). Another way of saying this is that '**income gearing** falls'.

If the **dividend per share** is held at the same level, **dividend cover** falls following conversion, thanks to the reduction in **earnings per share**.

Given the same share price, the **PE ratio** (see pages 30–1) would rise following conversion, again because of the reduction in **earnings per share**.

ConvertibleCo plc

CONSOLIDATED PROFIT AND LOSS ACCOUNT FOR THE YEAR ENDED 31 DECEMBER

	Before conversion		After conversion	
	£m	£m	£m	£m
TURNOVER		100.00		100.00
OPERATING PROFIT		12.00		12.00
less INTEREST PAYABLE				
BANK LOANS	1.20		1.20	
CONVERTIBLE BOND	0.80		–	
		2.00		1.20
PROFIT BEFORE TAX		10.00		10.80
less CORPORATION TAX		3.30		3.56
NET PROFIT AFTER TAX		6.70		7.24
less DIVIDENDS PAID		3.00		3.60
RETAINED PROFIT		3.70		3.64
No. of 50p shares in issue		20m		24m
Share price		700p		700p
Interest cover (times)		6		10
Earnings per share		33.50p		30.15p
Dividend per share		15.00p		15.00p
Dividend cover (times)		2.23		2.01
Yield		2.14%		2.14%
PE ratio		20.90		23.21

Raising money by issuing new shares

One of the events that significantly changes the appearance of a company's balance sheet is when money is raised for the business by creating and selling additional shares. There is a principle in British company law that new shares sold for cash should be offered first to the existing owners of the business, the shareholders. This is the principle of **pre-emption rights**. So the traditional way of marketing new shares for cash is via a **rights issue** – so called because the existing shareholders have the right to subscribe for the new shares, in proportion to their existing holdings.

Rights issues are somewhat cumbersome and expensive, however, so there is a tendency nowadays to use other methods such as the **placing and open offer**. In this case provisional buyers for the new shares are found among the big investing institutions. But there is an **open offer** to existing shareholders, who have the right to buy the new shares in place of the investing institutions if they want them. The legal requirements are thus satisfied. To the extent that existing shareholders take up this offer, the number of shares ending up with the institutions is reduced.

The process is easiest to illustrate with a **rights issue**, so we will take this as our example and to focus on the key points we will revert to the relatively simple accounts of the company that we started with: SimpleCo plc. So SimpleCo decides to create and issue, say, 2m new 50p shares. Since there are already 20m shares in issue, it offers these new shares to its existing shareholders in the ratio of one new share for every ten already held.

Typically, the new shares might be offered at a price around 20% below the market price of the existing shares (**at a discount** of 20% to the market price). This is to encourage shareholders to buy,

and so that the new shares will still be taken up even if the market price falls a bit between the date the price for the new shares is decided and the date when shareholders have to elect to buy. But the precise discount to the market price is not crucial, as long as all the existing shareholders are offered the same terms (this will become clearer later).

Suppose the market price of our company's shares is 700p and it decides to offer the new shares at 500p. This is a discount of rather more than 20% but it helps to illustrate the principle. Since 2m new shares are being issued, at a price of 500p the issue will raise £10m before costs.

Since this £10m is being raised by the issue of shares, it represents an addition to the shareholders' money in the business. So it is no surprise that SimpleCo's shareholders' funds overall rise by £10m after the issue (again, we're ignoring the expenses that crop up in practice). Of the 500p paid for each new share, only 50p represents the **nominal** or **par value** of the share, so 2m multiplied by 50p (making £1m in total) is added to **called up share capital**, increasing it to £11m. The remaining 450p of the 500p paid for each new share represents a **premium** over the par value, so 2m multiplied by 450p (or £9m in total) is added to **share premium account**, taking it up to £13m.

This records where the money came from. But what happens to the actual £10m in cash that the company raised? It can, of course, be used for any of the needs of the business. But in our example we have assumed that the company uses £7m to pay off its bank overdraft and the remaining £3m is deposited with the bank until it is needed, thereby boosting the company's cash resources. However, a rights issue has other ramifications, which we will examine in the example on pages 66–8.

Balance sheet
Raising money by issuing new shares

Of the £10m cash raised by the **rights issue**, £7m is used to repay the **short-term borrowings** (the bank overdraft) and the remaining £3m is held on deposit until needed, thereby increasing the **cash at bank** to £8m.

Net assets are increased by the £10m raised by the **rights issue**.

Shareholders' funds increase by the £10m raised by the **rights issue**. Of this amount, £1m represents the **nominal value** of the new shares issued. The remaining £9m represents the **premium** over nominal value and is therefore added to **share premium account**.

The company's **financial ratios** improve significantly following the injection of an additional £10m of **shareholders' money**. **Borrowings** are reduced and **gearing** falls substantially. As it happens, the **net asset value per share** also rises, since the new shares were sold for a price well above the existing NAV.

SimpleCo plc

CONSOLIDATED BALANCE SHEET AS AT 31 DECEMBER

	Without rights issue		With one-for-ten rights issue of 2m new shares at 500p to raise £10m	
	£m	£m	£m	£m
FIXED ASSETS				
TANGIBLE ASSETS		30		30
CURRENT ASSETS				
STOCKS	11		11	
DEBTORS	18		18	
CASH AT BANK	5		8	
	34		37	
CREDITORS (DUE WITHIN ONE YEAR)				
TRADE CREDITORS	14		14	
CORPORATION TAX	2		2	
PROPOSED DIVIDEND	2		2	
BANK OVERDRAFT	7		0	
	25		18	
NET CURRENT ASSETS/ (LIABILITIES)		9		19
TOTAL ASSETS LESS CURRENT LIABILITIES		39		49
CREDITORS (DUE AFTER ONE YEAR)		10		10
NET ASSETS		29		39
CAPITAL AND RESERVES				
CALLED UP SHARE CAPITAL	10		11	
SHARE PREMIUM ACCOUNT	4		13	
PROFIT AND LOSS ACCOUNT	15		15	
SHAREHOLDERS' FUNDS		29		39
Gross borrowings		17		10
Net borrowings		12		2
Gross gearing		58.6%		25.6%
Net gearing		41.4%		5.1%
NAV		145p		177p

How a rights issue affects the share price

When a company announces that it is making a **rights issue**, a certain time later you will see that the share price in the newspaper is marked **xr** which stands for **ex-rights**. This means that a buyer of the shares after that date does not acquire the right to **subscribe** for the new shares. That right remains with the seller. On the same day as the shares are marked 'xr' the market price is likely to have dropped below its previous day's level.

The reason is that the issue of new shares at below market price affects the value of the existing shares, though shareholders do not suffer from this. In our SimpleCo example, the share price before the issue was 700p. A shareholder who accepts the offer to subscribe for one new share at 500p for every ten that he held will end up with 11 shares. Of these, ten had been worth 700p each and the eleventh cost him 500p.

To calculate the average price for one share you take ten multiplied by 700p, which comes to 7,000p, then add the 500p paid for the new share to arrive at 7,500p. Divide this 7,500p by the 11 shares that the investor now has and you arrive at a new price of 681.82p per share. This is known as the **ex-rights price** and the stock market will, in fact, adjust prices down in this way when the shares go ex-rights. But the shareholder who subscribed for new shares has not suffered any loss in the overall value of his holding (see the table on page 67).

What about a shareholder who could not or did not accept the offer to buy the new shares? He started, say, with ten shares worth 7,000p in total and finds himself with ten shares worth only 6,818.2p after the price adjustment.

The answer is that the shareholder who does not take up the rights to the new shares can **sell these rights** to somebody else. The **value of the rights** will in theory be the difference between the ex-rights price (681.8p) and the subscription price for the new shares (500p), so it would be 181.8p in our example. The 181.8p that the investor receives from selling his rights compensates him for the fall in value of his original ten shares. In practice, the value of the rights can fluctuate a little more in the market than this might suggest, though the principle holds good.

Where companies use a **placing and open offer** (see previous spread) to market new shares, the subscription price of the new shares is usually much closer to the market price of the old ones than it is with a rights issue. However, shareholders who do not take up their entitlement to the new shares cannot sell this entitlement to anyone else.

The precise subscription price charged for new shares in a rights issue does not matter too much as long as they are offered to existing shareholders. Our company could equally well have raised £10m by offering existing shareholders two new shares at 250p (rather than one at 500p) for every ten shares that they held. The ex-rights **price adjustment mechanism** would have compensated in the same way. The press frequently describes a rights issue as 'generous' if the shares are offered at a price that is a long way below the market price, but this is nonsense. The company belongs to its shareholders and it cannot therefore offer them anything that they do not already own.

However, the price at which new shares are offered can affect the **return** that shareholders receive from the **dividend**. If SimpleCo pays the same rate of **dividend per share** after a rights issue as before it, and the new shares were issued below market price, this has the same effect as a small increase in the dividend. If the new shares are offered at a price way below the existing market price (at 250p rather than 500p,

Price adjustment mechanism

How a rights issue affects the share price

---

1 for 10 rights issue at 500p
(market price before issue = 700p)

Investor has 10 shares at 700p each	=	7,000p
Subscribes for 1 new share at 500p	=	500p
		────
Total for 11 shares	=	7,500p
New (ex-rights) price for 1 share	=	681.82p

Value of rights to one new share

Ex-rights price	=	681.82p
Less subscription price for new share	=	500p
		────
Value of rights	=	181.82p

Dividend yield assuming 15p per share dividend

At 700p price before rights issue	=	2.14%
At 681.82p price after rights issue	=	2.20%

2 for 10 rights issue at 250p
(market price before issue = 700p)

Investor has 10 shares at 700p each	=	7,000p
Subscribes for 2 new shares at 250p	=	500p
		────
Total for 12 shares	=	7,500p
New (ex-rights) price for 1 share	=	625p

Value of rights to one new share

Ex-rights price	=	625p
Less subscription price for new share	=	250p
		────
Value of rights	=	375p

Dividend yield assuming 15p per share dividend

At 700p price before rights issue	=	2.14%
At 625p price after rights issue	=	2.40%

say) and the dividend is held at its original level, this can have the effect of a significant dividend increase. Where the new shares are offered at a very low price, commentators talk of a **deep-discounted rights issue.**

Most rights issues are **underwritten** so that the company is sure of getting its money even if shareholders do not choose to take up the new shares. This means that a number of big investors (insurance companies, pension funds and the like) agree to buy at the subscription price any new shares not taken up by shareholders. Needless to say, these **underwriters** charge a significant fee for providing this insurance. However, deep-discounted rights issues are generally not underwritten, as there is little chance that the new shares will not be taken up.

Cartoon copyright Pressdram Limited 2002. Reproduced by permission.

Free shares? Not as good as it sounds

There are times when companies decide to issue new shares free to their existing shareholders, who often find the process confusing. This kind of share issue is known as a **scrip issue** and it is basically an *accounting technicality*. But shareholders who do not understand what is going on may get a shock when they see the effects on the company's accounts – or on the **market price** of their shares.

Look at it like this. After a company has been in operation for some years, ploughing back profit into the business each year, its **profit and loss account reserves** may have grown to a very large figure. Unless the company has raised capital by issuing large quantities of new shares along the way, the reserves may completely dwarf the figure for **called up share capital**.

Another effect is that the share price in the stock market may by now have grown very **heavy**. In other words with the growth of the company year by year, the price of one share is now many pounds. While this would not be unusual in many overseas markets, the British prefer to measure their share prices in pence and consider the price is getting a bit **heavy** when it edges up towards the 1,000p or £10 level.

One answer would be to **split** the shares. Our company has shares of 50p nominal value which stand in the market at 500p. It could simply split each existing 50p share into two new shares of 25p nominal value and the share price would adjust down to 250p in the market. A shareholder would be no better and no worse off. A share split, while it increases the number of shares in issue, does not however have the effect of increasing the issued share capital as a money amount.

But it is more common to achieve a similar effect by a **scrip issue** (also known as a **capitalisation issue** and sometimes – misleadingly – as a **free issue** or **bonus issue**). The reason these last two descriptions are misleading is that they suggest the company is giving the shareholders something for nothing – which it is not doing (and could not do) since they own the company already.

In a scrip issue, part of the company's reserves is simply used to **pay up** new shares, which are then distributed free to existing shareholders, *pro rata* with their holdings. Viewed less technically, part of the reserves is transmuted into share capital. The **reserves** thus decrease and the **nominal share capital** rises by an identical amount, so that there is no overall change to shareholders' funds.

If shareholders were given one new share for each share they held, they would end up with two shares where they had one previously. If the market price was 500p ahead of the issue, it might be expected to adjust down to 250p. Again, shareholders would be no better or worse off than they were before.

In our example, however, we have assumed that SimpleCo makes a one-for-two scrip issue. Thus a shareholder with two existing shares ends up with a total of three shares after the issue. We will look at the price adjustment mechanism on pages 74–5.

The point to note for the moment is the reduction from £15m to £10m in SimpleCo's **profit and loss account reserves** and the corresponding £5m rise in **issued capital** to £15m following the scrip issue.

Nothing else has changed, however. SimpleCo's **assets** and **liabilities** are exactly the same as they were before the issue. Nor has the total of shareholders' funds changed. It still stands at £29m. No new money has been raised and no money has been disbursed. The key balance sheet ratios remain unchanged with the exception of the **net assets per share** figure or **NAV**. This falls from 145p to 96.7p, since the same

Balance sheet

Free shares? Not as good as it sounds

A **scrip issue** does not raise cash for the company or involve any movements of cash. Nor does it have any other effect on the 'real world' of the assets that the company owns and the liabilities that need to be set against these assets. These all remain exactly as they were before the issue.

A scrip issue makes no difference to the total shareholders' money (**shareholders' funds**) in the business. It simply involves a reallocation from one category of shareholders' funds to another: from **reserves** to **called up share capital**.

In this example the scrip issue is in the proportion of one-for-two, so **issued capital** is increased by a half (or £5m) and the **profit and loss account reserves** correspondingly reduce by £5m.

The company's key balance sheet ratios are unaffected by the **scrip issue**, with the exception of the **net asset value per share (NAV)**. There are now 30m 50p shares in issue against 20m previously, so the £29m of **net assets** now has to be allocated over 30m shares. The result is a reduction in the **NAV** from 145p to 96.7p.

SimpleCo plc

CONSOLIDATED BALANCE SHEET AS AT 31 DECEMBER

	Before scrip issue		After one-for-two scrip issue	
	£m	£m	£m	£m
FIXED ASSETS				
TANGIBLE ASSETS		30		30
CURRENT ASSETS				
STOCKS	11		11	
DEBTORS	18		18	
CASH AT BANK	5		5	
	34		34	
CREDITORS (DUE WITHIN ONE YEAR)				
TRADE CREDITORS	14		14	
CORPORATION TAX	2		2	
PROPOSED DIVIDEND	2		2	
BANK OVERDRAFT	7		7	
	25		25	
NET CURRENT ASSETS/ (LIABILITIES)		9		9
TOTAL ASSETS LESS CURRENT LIABILITIES		39		39
CREDITORS (DUE AFTER ONE YEAR)		10		10
NET ASSETS		29		29
CAPITAL AND RESERVES				
CALLED UP SHARE CAPITAL		10		15
SHARE PREMIUM ACCOUNT		4		4
PROFIT AND LOSS ACCOUNT		15		10
SHAREHOLDERS' FUNDS		29		29
Gross borrowings		17		17
Net borrowings		12		12
Gross gearing		58.6%		58.6%
Net gearing		41.4%		41.4%
NAV		145p		96.7p

amount of net assets is now allocated to a larger number of shares.

We said earlier that a scrip issue made no difference to the value of a shareholder's interest in the company. There is, however, one exception. This is if 'free' shares are allocated to some shareholders but not to all of them. Many companies, for example, give their shareholders the option of taking their dividends as a scrip issue of shares rather than as a cash payment (a **scrip dividend**). In this case the shareholders who take the scrip shares rather than the cash are clearly increasing their proportionate stake in the company relative to those who do not.

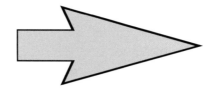

How scrip issues complicate comparisons

We have seen that a **scrip issue** is essentially an *accounting technicality*. But unfortunately it can and does cause complications for those who are monitoring company performance.

Let us start with the share price. Our example was of SimpleCo making a one-for-two scrip issue of 50p shares (this might also be described as a **50% capitalisation issue**, since the shareholder ended up with 50% more shares than he started with). An existing shareholder with two shares before the issue thus ended up with three shares.

We have seen that each shareholder still has the same proportionate stake in SimpleCo as he had before the scrip issue. Nor has the value of the company as a whole changed, since no cash was raised by the issue. The only change is that three shares now represent a value that was represented by only two shares before the issue. In other words, three shares after the issue are worth the same as two shares before it, and the market price of each share will **adjust** down to reflect this. In our example, the share price before the issue was 500p and two shares were therefore worth 1,000p. After the issue, three shares should be worth 1,000p so each share is now worth 333.3p (1,000p divided by three).

As with a rights issue, the stock exchange sets a date after which a buyer of the shares does not acquire the right to the new shares being issued via the scrip issue. This is the date on which, in our example, the share price in the market would adjust down from 500p to 333.3p. The share price will be marked **xc** meaning **ex-capitalisation** on this day and for a time afterwards. Remember that a **capitalisation issue** is just another term for a **scrip issue**.

Many shareholders who have not noticed that a scrip issue was taking place or who do not understand the mechanisms are aghast when they suddenly notice that the price of their shares has fallen by a third. What sort of trouble has the company got itself into? Their apprehension is totally unfounded. But the scrip issue does introduce other complications.

We saw on the previous spread that **net assets per share** (the **NAV** figure) will fall after the issue as the same amount of assets is now being spread over more shares. The same applies to **earnings**. If our company had earnings per share of 35p in the year before the scrip issue, this would be the equivalent of only 23.33p on the capital as increased by the issue. Likewise, a **dividend** of 15p per share net ahead of the issue would be the equivalent of 10p per share after the issue. If the company keeps its **dividend per share** at the old level of 15p on the increased number of shares, this represents in practice a very hefty dividend increase. The shareholder now gets 15p per share on three shares where he got it on only two before. If the company simply wants to maintain the shareholders' income constant, it would scale down the dividend per share from 15p to 10p after the issue. In our example we've assumed the company reduces the dividend per share from 15p to 12p. But in reality this still represents a significant increase (see page 75).

Whenever you are examining the historical trend of a company's **share price**, **earnings** or **dividend per share**, you need to be sure that all three have been adjusted for any scrip issues that have taken place. Most suppliers of financial information carry out this adjustment automatically, as do companies themselves when they present their five-year profit record. And when a commentator says that the company's dividend has increased to 15p compared with the **equivalent** of 10p or an **effective** 10p the previous year, he probably means that he has adjusted the previous year's figures for an intervening scrip issue.

Share prices in the stock market will adjust to reflect the **scrip issue** or **capitalisation issue**. The shares will be marked **xc** on the date the adjustment takes place.

To compare **earnings per share** in the years before the **scrip issue** with those after the issue has taken place, the older figures need to be restated in terms of the expanded share capital.

Dividends paid in the years before the **scrip issue** took place need to be adjusted to bring them on the same basis as payments declared after the scrip issue.

In our example, the company has cut its **dividend per share** between years three and four from 15p to 12p. But since the 12p is being paid on a larger number of shares, the **adjusted figures** show that the dividend has really been increased.

Had the company simply maintained its dividend per share at 15p after the scrip issue, this would have represented a true 50% increase in the payment.

Adjustments for a one-for-two scrip issue, when the market price of the shares ahead of the issue was 500p

SHARE PRICE ADJUSTMENT

Shareholder had 2 shares at 500p each before the issue = 1,000p
Shareholder has 3 shares after the issue. Total value = 1,000p
Therefore value of one share after the issue is $\dfrac{1,000p}{3} = 333.3p$

EARNINGS ADJUSTMENT

Over a three-year period the company has published the following **earnings per share** figures. After the end of year three, it makes a one-for-two scrip issue, then publishes earnings of 28p per share for year four:

		eps as published at the time
YEAR	1	25p
YEAR	2	30p
YEAR	3	35p
		one-for-two scrip
YEAR	4	28p

However, the earnings for year four are spread over 50% more shares than the earnings for earlier years. To express those earnings of earlier years in terms of today's capital, as enlarged by the scrip issue, you need to reduce them to two-thirds of the figures shown above:

		eps as published at the time	eps adjusted for scrip issue
YEAR	1	25p	16.7p
YEAR	2	30p	20.0p
YEAR	3	35p	23.3p
		one-for-two scrip	
YEAR	4	28p	28p

The adjusted figures now give a true picture of the company's progress and should be used in any comparisons of one year with another.

DIVIDEND ADJUSTMENT

For valid comparisons, past dividends need to be adjusted for scrip issues in exactly the same way as earnings. The dividends paid before the one-for-two issue must be adjusted as shown:

		Dividend as published at the time	Dividend adjusted for scrip issue
YEAR	1	10.0p	6.7p
YEAR	2	12.5p	8.3p
YEAR	3	15.0p	10.0p
		one-for-two scrip	
YEAR	4	12.0p	12.0p

How use of borrowed money affects performance

The financial **gearing** of a company is one of the first things that any user of accounts will look at. It can tell you a lot about the degree of risk in a company's financial structure.

Balance sheet gearing is, as we have seen, the relationship between **borrowed money** and **shareholders' money** in a business (see pages 26–7). **Income gearing** is the relationship between the profits the company earns and the interest charges that have to be set against those profits (see pages 8–9). The two are, of course, different sides of the same coin. A company that uses a lot of borrowed money is likely to have higher interest charges than one that does not.

Companies can use borrowed money to improve or **gear up** the returns to their shareholders when things are going well. But when the company's trading hits problems, gearing will have exactly the opposite effect. It is a two-edged sword in the finance director's armoury.

To illustrate the principle, we've abandoned the companies we have been using for illustration so far and taken a more extreme example. This shows abbreviated profit statements for two very differently structured companies.

The example on page 77 – 'Level of gearing' – shows how these two companies might fare in good times and bad. One has very high **income gearing**. There are interest charges of £60m to set against its operating profits of £100m before arriving at the pre-tax profit of £40m. The **interest cover** is thus only 1.67 times.

The other company has relatively low **income gearing**. There are interest charges of only £5m to set against its operating profits of £45m before arriving at the pre-tax profit of £40m. **Interest cover** is 9 times.

Note that both companies have exactly the same **pre-tax profit** of £40m at the outset. Then assume that both encounter very buoyant trading conditions and both register a 50% *increase* in operating profits.

In the case of our **high-geared company**, this takes operating profits up from £100m to £150m. But the interest charges on borrowed money remain unchanged at £60m. The effect is that the **profit before tax** shoots up from £40m to £90m – a rise of 125% – and the effect on **earnings** for shareholders would be roughly similar. The gearing is working very much in the shareholders' favour.

Meantime, our **low-geared company** also sees its operating profits rise by 50% from £45m to £67.5m. But with the much lower level of interest charges, the **pre-tax profit** rises by only 56%-odd for the 50% rise in operating profits. Shareholders are deriving some benefit from the gearing, but it is fairly minor.

Now see what happens to our two companies, from their original starting positions, if they hit trading problems and each suffers a 50% fall in **operating profits**. In the case of the **high-geared company** the operating profits fall from £100m to £50m, where they no longer cover interest charges of £60m. The company is forced into a £10m loss before tax.

Our **low-geared company** is also hit. But in this case the fairly modest income gearing merely translates a 50% fall in **operating profits** into a fall of 56%-odd in **pre-tax profits**. The company has suffered a sharp setback but it is nowhere near making a loss.

Thus, gearing works in favour of shareholders in good times and against them in bad. There is no such thing as a 'right' level of gearing. It depends very much on the nature of the company's operations and whether they are likely to involve big fluctuations in profitability from one year to the next. But remember that there is also no such thing as a free lunch. **High gearing** may look clever in a boom, but it greatly increases the risks if boom turns to slump. And, ultimately, companies which cannot pay their interest charges go bust.

The company on the left has **high income gearing**, with interest charges on borrowed money absorbing more than half of available profits. By contrast, the company on the right has relatively small interest charges and **low income gearing**. But in both cases profits before tax amount to £40m.

When profits are rising, the **high-geared company** does better for its shareholders than the **low-geared** one, with profits before tax rising more than twice as fast as operating profits.

When profits are falling, the dangers of **high income gearing** are all too apparent. A 50% drop in operating profits is enough to turn our **high-geared company** into loss. The **low-geared company** shows its better defensive qualities in these circumstances. The same percentage fall in operating profits is not nearly as serious.

EFFECTS OF GEARING

LEVEL OF GEARING

		High-geared company £m	High-geared company % rise or fall	Low-geared company £m	Low-geared company % rise or fall
Starting position	OPERATING PROFIT	100		45	
	INTEREST PAYABLE	60		5	
	PROFIT BEFORE TAX	40		40	
Operating profits rise by 50%	OPERATING PROFIT	150	+50%	67.5	+50%
	INTEREST PAYABLE	60		5.0	
	PROFIT BEFORE TAX	90	+125%	62.5	+56%
Operating profits fall by 50%	OPERATING PROFIT	50	−50%	22.5	−50%
	INTEREST PAYABLE	60		5.0	
	PROFIT BEFORE TAX	−10	*loss*	17.5	−56%

The profit repercussions when interest rates move

It is not only the level of borrowings that affects the way a company's earnings respond to good and bad times. The type of borrowings is also vital. Companies may borrow money either at **fixed rates of interest** or **floating rates of interest**.

When a company borrows at fixed rates of interest (say, by issuing a long-term **fixed-interest bond**) it at least knows what level of interest it will be paying on this money for many years ahead. On the other hand, if it issued this bond when rates for fixed-interest money were high, it is committed to paying a high rate of interest for many years, even if interest rates fall. Others who borrow later may get their money more cheaply.

If the company borrows at **floating rates of interest**, the interest rate that it pays will rise or fall in line with the general level of interest rates in the economy. The company will benefit if interest rates subsequently fall and suffer if they rise. The rate of interest on floating rate loans for large companies is usually linked to the **London Inter Bank Offered Rate** or **LIBOR**. This LIBOR is a measure of the cost of money to the banks themselves and it is constantly changing with supply and demand. It is a benchmark for short-term interest rates in the economy. The rate is normally expressed in **basis points**; there are 100 basis points to one **percentage point**. A rate of interest set at 60 basis points over LIBOR would therefore cost 5.6% if LIBOR itself was 5% at the time.

Thus, if LIBOR falls on average over a period, the rate of interest the borrower pays on a LIBOR-linked loan will also fall. Conversely, if LIBOR rises, the borrower will find himself paying more interest (perhaps much more) than he had expected at the outset.

To summarise: companies that borrow at **fixed rates** know what they will be paying but may find later they have paid too much. Companies that borrow at **floating rates** will benefit when interest rates fall but may suffer badly when they rise.

Therefore, if you are looking at a company's borrowings you need to see whether they are taken at fixed or floating rates of interest, or a mix. The notes to the accounts should show this.

Our example on page 79 again takes an extreme case to illustrate the point. It shows how a moderately **high-geared** company which borrows floating rate money is at risk to changes in interest rates as well as to fluctuations in its profits. In our hypothetical case, we've assumed for convenience a 10% interest rate as the starting point. A subsequent five percentage point *rise* in interest rates can reduce the company's profits before tax by 25%. The other side of the coin is that its profits will be boosted by a comparable *fall* in interest rates.

If the rise in interest rates coincides (as it quite often does) with difficult trading conditions and falling operating profits, the company may be in trouble.

The company on the left, with **fixed-rate borrowings**, is not affected by the rise in short-term interest rates. But neither does it benefit when they fall.

You need to be a little careful in analysing borrowings. Companies may borrow floating-rate money but protect themselves in one way or another against the effect of rising interest rates. One way is to buy a **cap**, which is a form of insurance policy that compensates the borrower if interest rates rise above a certain point. Another is to **swap** the floating-rate debt for fixed-rate, in which case the company pays a fixed rate of interest even though it initially borrowed floating-rate money.

Interest rate **hedges** of this kind are becoming increasingly common. They fall under the general description of **derivative** financial products. The notes to the accounts and/or the finance director's report should make clear to what extent the company uses them, though the position is not always as transparent as it should be.

The company on the left borrows money only at **fixed rates of interest**. It is therefore unaffected when interest rates subsequently rise, but neither does it benefit when they fall. The company on the right will see its interest charge fall or rise with changes in the general level of **short-term interest rates** in the economy. For illustration we are assuming an interest rate of 10% as the starting position.

When **short-term interest rates** fall significantly there is a big boost to the profits of the company on the right, which borrowed **floating-rate** money and now pays only 5%. The company on the left, which borrowed at **fixed rates**, does not benefit.

It is when interest rates rise sharply that the dangers of borrowing **floating-rate money** become apparent. The company on the right (now paying 15%) suffers a 25% fall in profits. The one on the left, with **fixed-rate borrowings**, does not run this risk.

EFFECTS OF GEARING

MOVEMENTS IN INTEREST RATES

		Company with all borrowings at fixed rates of interest		Company with all borrowings at floating rates of interest	
		£m	% rise or fall	£m	% rise or fall
Starting position	OPERATING PROFIT	300		300	
	INTEREST PAYABLE (at 10%)	100		100	
	PROFIT BEFORE TAX	200		200	
Interest rates fall by 5 percentage points	OPERATING PROFIT	300		300	
	INTEREST PAYABLE	100		50	
	PROFIT BEFORE TAX	200	0%	250	+25%
Interest rates rise by 5 percentage points	OPERATING PROFIT	300		300	
	INTEREST PAYABLE	100		150	
	PROFIT BEFORE TAX	200	0%	150	−25%

How use of borrowed money affects asset values

We have looked at the way that the **financial gearing** of a company can affect its profit performance in differing circumstances. But the relationship between **shareholders' money** and **borrowed money** in a business has another important consequence: its effect on **asset values**. It is the balance sheet that we now need to look at.

Though most companies are valued in the stock market according to the profits that they earn or are thought capable of earning, there are some companies that are valued on a rather different basis. These are companies which own large quantities of **readily saleable assets**, on which it is easy to put a market value. Typical examples are companies whose main business is owning commercial real estate which is held as a long-term investment (**property investment companies**) and companies which exist to hold shares in other companies as an investment (**investment trusts**). The share prices of both these types of company are generally determined more by the market value of the assets that they own than by their earnings.

Other types of company may also own large quantities of **readily saleable assets** and, though this is not their main business, the value of these assets can still have an influence on the share price. Typical examples are retail groups that own the properties from which they operate or leisure and catering groups owning large quantities of pubs.

As we've seen earlier, most **fixed assets** are shown in company accounts at what they cost, less an allowance for wear and tear (**depreciation**). However, assets in which there is a ready market are more likely to be shown at **market values**. In the case of commercial real estate – offices, shops or factories – which companies use in their own business, they have a choice in the UK. They may show these properties in their accounts at depreciated cost or they may periodically **revalue** them to market values. The notes to the accounts will make it clear which method is adopted.

Where a company's shares are valued wholly or partly by reference to the value of the assets that it owns, the **net asset value per share (NAV)** becomes all-important. And the rise or fall in the NAV is in turn strongly affected by the gearing of the company.

Take a look at the example on page 81. To illustrate the point we've invented two different companies and shown an abbreviated form of their balance sheets. We've assumed that both are companies that own real estate as their main business. Each starts off with **net assets** of £100m and a **net asset value per share (NAV)** of 100p. But the **ungeared** company uses no borrowed money at all. It runs its business entirely on shareholders' money. The **high-geared** company, on the other hand, uses as much borrowed money as shareholders' money. In other words, borrowings are equal to 100% of shareholders' funds and the net asset value of £100m is arrived at after deducting loans of £100m. Though both have the same **net assets**, the high-geared company actually owns properties worth twice as much as those of the ungeared company.

Now assume that the commercial real estate market is booming and each company commissions a revaluation of the properties that it owns. And assume for convenience that both revaluations disclose that property values have risen by 40%. Our **ungeared** company sees the value of its properties rise from £100m to £140m and the **high-geared** company sees its property values up from £200m to £280m.

Now look at the different impact on the value of net assets. In the case of the ungeared company, the **net asset value** has simply risen by the same percentage amount as the properties: 40%. With the high-geared company the **net asset value** has risen by 80% for the same 40% rise in the value of the properties. The gearing in the company's financial structure is magnifying the effect of

	Ungeared company			High-geared company		
	Before property revaluation	After property revaluation	Percentage change	Before property revaluation	After property revaluation	Percentage change
	£m	£m		£m	£m	
Assets						
Land and buildings	100	140	+40%	200	280	+40%
Liabilities						
Borrowed money	0	0		100	100	
Net assets	100	140	+40%	100	180	+80%
Represented by						
Called up share capital						
(50p shares)	50	50		50	50	
Share premium account	30	30		30	30	
Revaluation reserve	0	40		0	80	
Profit and loss account	20	20		20	20	
Shareholders' funds	100	140	+40%	100	180	+80%
Borrowings as % of						
shareholders' funds	0%	0%		100%	56%	
Number of shares in issue	100m	100m		100m	100m	
Net asset value per share	100p	140p	+40%	100p	180p	+80%

rising property values for the benefit of the shareholders. The net asset value per share has risen to 180p, whereas it has risen only to 140p in the case of the ungeared company. You would expect to see the share price of the high-geared company increasing faster in the stock market than the price of the ungeared company.

Note, too, that we are meeting a new type of reserve for the first time, under the general heading of shareholders' funds. This is the **revaluation reserve**, to which the uplift in the value of the properties is allocated.

The sort of balance-sheet gearing that we've illustrated here is fine in good times, when **asset values** are rising. But there's another side to the coin. If asset values are falling, the net asset value of our high-geared company will fall faster than that of the ungeared company. In a real property market crash where the value of commercial real estate halved, our high-geared company would be left with no net assets at all and would probably be wiped out. Our ungeared company would see its NAV halve, but would survive.

Even where a company itself undertakes no formal revaluation of its assets, investment analysts and other commentators will often make their own estimates of what the assets are really worth and what effect this would have on the NAV.

You will also see that the question of asset value arises frequently in **takeover battles** on the stock exchange. The company under siege will often commission a revaluation of its properties to produce an increase in its **NAV**. This, in turn, will be used to argue that the value of the takeover offer is too low, and that it should be rejected.

'Death, War — meet Accountancy.'

Cartoon reproduced by permission of The Spectator.

When control of working capital is lost

Ready money – we'll call it **cash**, though obviously it includes money held at the bank – is the lifeblood of business. A company that allows it to drain away may not be around for very long. But it's all too easy for a company to take its eye off the ball and allow its precious cash to be soaked up in non-productive ways. To illustrate this we've reverted to our original company, SimpleCo. It's not in too bad shape. It has £5m of **cash** in the bank and its **net gearing**, though not low, is a containable 41%.

Now assume that it takes its eye off the ball and its **cash management** becomes slack. The company does not chase those who owe it money sufficiently vigorously for payment. It ceases to bargain sufficiently hard on the credit terms from its own suppliers. And it ceases to monitor sufficiently closely the level of stocks that it needs to hold. Its financial position can deteriorate almost overnight.

Take the **stocks** question first. Stock levels at the company have risen dramatically from £11m to £16m. This means that it has had to use £5m of its cash in buying extra stocks. If a company's business is expanding rapidly it may need to invest in larger volumes of stocks in order to be able to satisfy its expanding customer list. But unless there is evidence of rapidly expanding turnover, a rise such as this in the stocks level might sound a warning note. Is the company holding larger stocks of raw materials than it needs? Worse still, is it allowing stocks of finished goods to pile up; goods that it has not yet been able to sell?

Now look at the figure for **debtors**. It has risen by £7m to £25m. Remember that this is mainly money that is owing to our company for goods or services that it has supplied and for which it has not yet been paid. Our company has effectively extended additional interest-free loans of £7m to its customers and this is money that has to come out of its own cash resources. Again, if there were evidence of rapidly increasing turnover, a rise in the amounts owing by customers might be expected. But without this evidence the situation is worrying.

Next look at **trade creditors**, under the heading **creditors (due within one year)**. If the company's business were expanding rapidly we might expect to see the figures for **stocks**, **debtors** and **creditors** rising roughly in step. But creditors have actually fallen slightly from £14m to £13m. There has therefore been a small reduction in what are effectively interest-free loans from suppliers. Again, this reduces the cash that our company has available.

The effect of these changes, taken together, is that our company has used up all but £1m of the £5m **cash** that it previously held in the bank. It is in danger of running out of cash for its day-to-day needs. Almost worse, it has had to borrow a further £9m from the bank, which takes the **bank overdraft** up from £7m to £16m. It is surprising that the banks have allowed it to go thus far. They must be becoming seriously worried.

The banks are unlikely to want to lend more when they look at the effect of these changes on the company's **gearing**. Net borrowings have risen from £12m to £25m and **net gearing** is up from 41% to a worrying 86%. And as a result SimpleCo faces much higher **interest costs**.

Of course, the answer is for **SimpleCo** to regain control over its **stocks** and **debtors** (if it can!), get the figures down to release the cash that the business needs. But this will take time and if cash needs are pressing and the banks are unwilling to help further, the company might need to ask its shareholders to put up more cash to bail it out of its difficulties. But shareholders will not be too happy at the thought of putting up cash for new shares via a **rights issue**, simply to get SimpleCo out of trouble that it should not have got into in the first place.

If the company is listed on the stock exchange, the chances are that its share price has been falling rapidly as its problems have surfaced. The way might be open for a financially stronger competitor to snap it up on the cheap via an opportunistic **takeover bid**.

FINANCIAL RATIOS CAN DETERIORATE RAPIDLY WHEN A COMPANY ALLOWS ITS STOCKS AND DEBTORS TO GET OUT OF HAND

The right-hand column shows how SimpleCo has tied up large amounts of **cash** by buying larger quantities of **stocks** and extending more **credit** to customers – the **trade debtors**. The result has been to soak up the cash holdings and require a large increase in **short-term borrowings**.

SimpleCo has been unable to secure an increase in **trade credit** – effectively, interest-free loans from its suppliers. In fact, the figure for **creditors** has fallen. So there is no relief here from the pressure on its own cash resources.

SimpleCo has more than doubled the size of its **bank overdraft** to provide the cash to finance the higher levels of stocks and debtors. The company's bankers must be getting worried, and it might have problems in persuading them to lend any more.

The higher **borrowings** mean that a key financial ratio – the company's gearing – has taken a severe turn for the worse. **Net gearing** (borrowings less cash, expressed as a percentage of shareholders' funds) is now up to 86%.

SimpleCo plc
CONSOLIDATED BALANCE SHEET AS AT 31 DECEMBER

	Starting position		With poor cash management	
	£m	£m	£m	£m
FIXED ASSETS				
TANGIBLE ASSETS		30		30
CURRENT ASSETS				
STOCKS	11		16	
DEBTORS	18		25	
CASH AT BANK	5		1	
	34		42	
CREDITORS (DUE WITHIN ONE YEAR)				
TRADE CREDITORS	14		13	
CORPORATION TAX	2		2	
PROPOSED DIVIDEND	2		2	
BANK OVERDRAFT	7		16	
	25		33	
NET CURRENT ASSETS/(LIABILITIES)		9		9
TOTAL ASSETS LESS CURRENT LIABILITIES		39		39
CREDITORS (DUE AFTER ONE YEAR)		10		10
NET ASSETS		29		29
CAPITAL AND RESERVES				
CALLED UP SHARE CAPITAL	10		10	
SHARE PREMIUM ACCOUNT	4		4	
PROFIT AND LOSS ACCOUNT	15		15	
SHAREHOLDERS' FUNDS		29		29
Number of 50p shares in issue (m)		20		20
Gross borrowings (£m)		17		26
Net borrowings (£m)		12		25
Gross gearing (%)		59%		90%
Net gearing (%)		41%		86%

Mechanics of the takeover bid

When one company tries to **take over** another on the stock exchange there will generally be a lot of argument and discussion about the relative values of the two companies. This will involve frequent references to different features in the accounts. And after a takeover has taken place, the accounts of the company making the bid will be radically altered. For both these reasons we need to take a look at the takeover process. We'll refer to the company making the takeover bid as the **bidder** and the company it seeks to acquire as the **target**: call them BidderCo and TargetCo.

The purpose of a takeover is for the bidder to acquire control and ownership of the target company. The bidder can get control by acquiring more than 50% of the **votes** in the target. As most companies have a one-vote-per-ordinary-share structure, this normally involves acquiring over 50% of the ordinary shares of the target. The bidder would have control with only 50.01% of the votes of his target, but he would have nothing like full ownership as this would leave **minority shareholders** in the target owning the remaining 49.99%. The object of most (but not all) takeovers is to acquire all the shares of the target and assume total ownership.

The target company then becomes a **wholly-owned subsidiary** of the bidder. To make it easier for a bidder to acquire the remaining shares in the target when he has already gained control of an overwhelming majority, there is some help from English company law. A bidder who acquires as much as 90% of the shares that he bid for may **compulsorily acquire** the remaining 10%.

Though the recipient of a takeover bid is often referred to as the 'victim' company, it is by no means invariably an unwilling victim. A company's directors might think that it makes sense, and is to the benefit of their shareholders, to be taken over by a larger and stronger concern and would negotiate suitable terms. But this is not the last word. It is ultimately up to the shareholders of the target company to decide whether or not they want to dispose of their shares to the bidder. The directors of the target company may advise their shareholders to accept or reject a bid, but it is the shareholders who decide.

Normally a would-be bidder will approach the directors of the intended target company and at least try to get their support for the proposed bid. If the target's board agrees, it will become an **agreed bid** (though the shareholders still have to agree!). If the target's directors reject the bid approach but the bidder decides to press ahead regardless by appealing direct to shareholders, then it becomes a **hostile bid**. If more than one bidder tries to gain control of the same target it becomes a **contested bid**. The conduct of takeovers in London is governed by a non-statutory body, the **Panel on Takeovers and Mergers**, which publishes its more important rules as a **Takeover Code**.

The bidder also has a choice of currencies that it can offer to the target's shareholders in return for their own shares. It can, of course, offer **cash**. In this case, if the target's shareholders accept, they simply take the money and run. They have no continuing interest in the fortunes of the combined group after the takeover. And, for tax purposes, they will have sold their shares and might be liable for **capital gains tax**.

Alternatively, the bidder might offer to swap its own **shares** for the shares in the target. This would be referred to as a **paper bid**. The bidder creates the necessary number of new shares and exchanges them in the agreed ratio for the target company's shares. In this case the value of the bid will depend on the bidder's share price in the market. If the target company's shareholders accept, they retain an interest in the fortunes of the combined group, in which they have become shareholders.

There are variations on these themes. The bidder might offer a mix of shares and cash or

CONSOLIDATED PROFIT AND LOSS ACCOUNT FOR YEAR ENDED 31 DECEMBER				
	BEFORE THE BID		**AFTER THE BID**	
	BidderCo	TargetCo	CombinedCo (assuming 7 for 5 share bid)	CombinedCo (assuming £70m cash bid)
	£m	£m	£m	£m
TURNOVER	100.0	80.0	180.0	180.0
OPERATING PROFIT	12.0	6.0	18.0	18.0
less INTEREST PAYABLE	2.0	1.0	3.0	9.3
PROFIT BEFORE TAX	10.0	5.0	15.0	8.7
less CORPORATION TAX	3.0	1.5	4.5	2.6
NET PROFIT AFTER TAX	7.0	3.5	10.5	6.1
less DIVIDENDS PAID	3.0	1.5	5.1	3.0
RETAINED PROFIT	4.0	2.0	5.4	3.1
Shares in issue (m)	20.0	10.0	34.0	20.0
Earnings per share (p)	35.0	35.0	30.9	30.5
Dividends per share (p)	15.0	15.0	15.0	15.0
Operating profit margin (%)	12.0	7.5	10.0	10.0
Pre-tax profit margin (%)	10.0	6.3	8.3	4.8
Interest cover (times)	6.0	6.0	6.0	1.9
Dividend cover (times)	2.3	2.3	2.1	2.0

perhaps offer other types of security (like **loans** or **convertible stocks**) in place of shares. And a paper offer might include a **cash alternative**. The important point is that the structure of the bid will dictate the shape of the combined group's accounts after the merger.

To illustrate the mechanics of a bid and their effects, we've assumed that BidderCo (in fact it is identical to our original SimpleCo company) makes a takeover offer for another company – TargetCo – exactly half its own size. In other words, all its accounts items (except for turnover – we will see why later) are half the size of the corresponding ones for BidderCo. And the total value of the company in the stock market (its **market capitalisation**) before the bid is announced

as half that of BidderCo. Let us assume that BidderCo's share price is 500p.

Now, the first point to note in most takeovers is that the bidder has to offer a price for the shares in its target that is significantly above target's market price at the time of the offer. Why, otherwise, should target's shareholders accept? Let us assume in our example that TargetCo's directors bargain hard and persuade Original's directors to offer a price of 700p per TargetCo share as the price of their recommendation. Since TargetCo has 10m 50p shares in issue, this means that BidderCo will be paying £70m for the whole company.

Let's assume first that BidderCo is bidding in **shares**. These are worth 500p in the market at the time and it needs to offer shares worth 700p for each TargetCo share. It can achieve this by offering seven of its own shares for every five in TargetCo. Seven BidderCo shares are worth 3,500p. Divide this by five and it values each TargetCo share at 700p. This works out at £70m for the whole company, since TargetCo has 10m shares in issue. The precise value of the bid will, of course, vary if BidderCo's own share price moves up or down.

Look at the profit and loss account and key ratios of the two companies before the bid and then look at the result of putting the two companies together after a share bid. Remember that for convenience we've assumed that all TargetCo's figures were exactly half those of BidderCo, with the exception of **turnover**, which is more than half.

Right down to the level of net profit after tax we can simply add the figures of the two companies together to arrive at the corresponding figure for the combined group. But though the £10.50m figure for **net profit** is 50% higher than that for BidderCo alone, it has to be spread over more than 50% more shares. This is because BidderCo had to offer more than one of its own shares for each TargetCo share. The result is that earnings per share have fallen from 35p for BidderCo alone to 30.9p for the combined group. Commentators will refer to this as **earnings dilution**. And if the same 15p per share **dividend** is paid on the enlarged capital after the bid, the cost will be more than 50% higher than the dividend for BidderCo, with the result that **dividend cover** also falls.

Why did BidderCo launch a takeover bid that resulted in earnings dilution, at least in the short run? One answer could lie in TargetCo's **profit margins**. Ahead of the bid, TargetCo's pre-tax profits represented only 6.25% of its turnover whereas BidderCo had pre-tax profit margins of 10%. If BidderCo could get TargetCo's profit margins up to its own level, the earnings dilution would be more than eliminated. BidderCo may be reckoning that economies of scale and the elimination of duplicated costs will allow it to get the same profit margins from the TargetCo business as it does from its own.

Suppose now that BidderCo decides to bid in

cash instead of shares and that it borrows from the banks the whole of the £70m needed to make the bid. In this case the profit and loss account for the combined group will look rather different (see extreme right-hand column). We've assumed that BidderCo has to pay an interest rate of 9% on the £70m that it borrows. You will see immediately that the **interest charge** shoots up to £9.30m, reducing interest cover to just under twice. This has the effect of reducing pre-tax profits to £2.61m. While, as a result, the tax charge is lower, **net profit** is still also a lot lower at £6.09m.

Remember, however, that BidderCo has not issued any new shares. This means that earnings are spread only over the original 20m shares. There is **earnings dilution**, but it is not so very different from the earnings dilution resulting from the paper bid. The **dividend**, likewise, is payable only on the original 20m shares, so its cost is still £3m. If BidderCo can improve TargetCo's **profit margins** rapidly and squeeze improved earnings out of the business it has taken over, its shareholders might benefit more from the cash bid than the paper one. The improvement in earnings will be concentrated on a smaller number of shares, and earnings per share could therefore rise more rapidly.

There is one complication that we have so far ignored. Remember that BidderCo was paying £70m for the whole of TargetCo. But TargetCo had assets of only £14.5m so BidderCo was paying £55.5m for the **goodwill** of the business, over and above the value of the assets. What happens to this goodwill? The normal accounting rule nowadays is that goodwill acquired in this way is included in the accounts of the combined group as an **intangible asset** – you'll see the picture when we come to look at the balance sheet. Does the goodwill then have to be **depreciated** or **amortised** (the two words mean much the same) in the same way as a physical asset? Does a deduction have to be made from profits each year to recognise that goodwill 'wears out' in the same way as machines and vehicles wear out?

This is a difficult issue and we will not explore the intricacies here. But the general rule is that goodwill has to be depreciated (though over a long period) unless it can be demonstrated that in practice it is rising in value or at least holding its value. Different companies adopt different treatments.

If our company had to depreciate the goodwill each year after the merger, this would significantly reduce its **operating profit** (remember that depreciation is one of the deductions made before arriving at operating profit). It might reduce the published figure by, say, £2m and this would lead to a big reduction in **earnings per share**. So you will find that a lot of companies that do provide depreciation on goodwill (and thereby reduce their published earnings) will also give a figure for what earnings would have been without the goodwill depreciation. If the company itself does not do this, investment analysts and other commentators will often calculate this figure for themselves, and it is the earnings figure before depreciation of goodwill that is likely to be used in most discussions of the figures, to make it easier to compare one company with another on a like-for-like basis.

It is partly because of the different treatments of goodwill that another measure of company profits has gained in popularity, particularly in the United States. This is **EBITDA** or **earnings before interest, taxes, depreciation and amortisation**. It allows comparison of profit performance, particularly across national frontiers, without the distortion introduced by different levels of gearing and different taxation and accounting regimes.

What the bid does to balance sheet ratios

After the **takeover** of TargetCo by BidderCo, the most immediately obvious change to the balance sheet is the appearance under fixed assets of a figure of £55.50m for the **goodwill** acquired by BidderCo in the course of the bid. Aside from this item, the shape of the combined balance sheet depends very much on whether BidderCo bid in shares or in cash.

Take the **shares bid** first. In its new incarnation as CombinedCo, BidderCo's **share capital** has risen from £10m (or 20m 50p shares) to £17m (or 34m 50p shares). At the same time the **share premium account** has risen to £67m, reflecting the issue of 14m new shares at a **premium** of 450p to their par value of 50p. **Shareholders' funds** as a whole are up from £29m to £99m, since the £70m purchase of TargetCo was financed entirely by the issue of shares. BidderCo has taken on board the cash and the borrowings of TargetCo, but has not borrowed any additional money.

On the face of it, the result of combining the two companies has been to reduce **net gearing** (net borrowings as a percentage of shareholders' funds – see pages 26–7) from 41% to 18% because of the large increase in **shareholders' funds** following the share issue. Likewise, **net assets** are up from £29m to £99m and the **net asset value per share** has risen from 145p to 291p. But these figures hold good only if goodwill is treated as a 'real' asset. If you strip out **intangible assets** – and many investment analysts would do this – **net tangible assets** are only £43.5m after deducting the £55.5m of goodwill. Net tangible assets per share then reduce to 128p and the net gearing remains at its earlier level.

If BidderCo bid in **cash** for TargetCo, the outstanding feature of the balance sheet after the two companies come together is the massive rise to £74.50m in the combined group's **borrowings**, resulting from the £70m of term loans taken on to cover the purchase price. This enormous injection of debt, without any corresponding increase in shareholders' money, sends **net gearing** shooting up to over 300%. CombinedCo will need to reduce its gearing pretty rapidly. It might do this by selling off for cash parts of the TargetCo business that are not essential. Or it might make a **rights issue** to boost shareholders' funds. Or both.

Meantime, the question of goodwill again complicates the calculations. If the £55.5m of goodwill is removed from the equation, CombinedCo is shown to have negative tangible net assets and therefore a negative net tangible asset value per share. Likewise, there is no sensible way of calculating gearing. You cannot calculate borrowings as a percentage of shareholders' funds when there are no shareholders' funds after the removal of the goodwill.

The method of dealing with goodwill in company accounts is not wholly satisfactory, but unfortunately there is no completely satisfactory way. Goodwill which a company pays for by takeover is shown in the accounts, but goodwill that a company creates for itself is not. Clearly, BidderCo was worth a great deal more than the mere value of its assets before the takeover bid. The shares were valued in the stock market at 500p whereas the NAV was only 145p per share. The difference between the two is the value that investors in the stock market were prepared to put on BidderCo's business and profit-earning capacity, over and above the value of its assets. But this value, which BidderCo had created by building up a successful business, did not appear in its accounts.

The value of a company in the stock market is known as the **market capitalisation**. You arrive at this by multiplying the total number of shares in issue by the share price, and the market capitalisation may be quoted in the prices pages of newspapers. Thus, before the takeover bid BidderCo had 20m 50p shares in issue and the share price in the market was 500p. So BidderCo's market capitalisation at this point was 20m multiplied by 500p, or £100m. The market capitalisation is useful in getting an idea of the relative size of different companies.

CONSOLIDATED BALANCE SHEET AS AT 31 DECEMBER

	BEFORE THE BID		AFTER THE BID	
	BidderCo	TargetCo	CombinedCo (assuming 7 for 5 share bid)	CombinedCo (assuming £70m cash bid)
	£m	£m	£m	£m
FIXED ASSETS				
TANGIBLE ASSETS	30.0	15.0	45.0	45.0
INTANGIBLE ASSETS (GOODWILL)			55.5	55.5
CURRENT ASSETS				
STOCKS	11.0	5.5	16.5	16.5
DEBTORS	18.0	9.0	27.0	27.0
CASH AT BANK	5.0	2.5	7.5	7.5
	34.0	17.0	51.0	51.0
CREDITORS (DUE WITHIN ONE YEAR)				
TRADE CREDITORS	14.0	7.0	21.0	21.0
CORPORATION TAX	2.0	1.0	3.0	3.0
PROPOSED DIVIDEND	2.0	1.0	3.0	3.0
BANK OVERDRAFT	7.0	3.5	10.5	10.5
	25.0	12.5	37.5	37.5
NET CURRENT ASSETS/(LIABILITIES)	9.0	4.5	13.5	13.5
TOTAL ASSETS LESS CURRENT LIABILITIES	39.0	19.5	114.0	114.0
CREDITORS (DUE AFTER ONE YEAR)				
9% DEBENTURE STOCK 2009	7.0	3.5	10.5	10.5
TERM LOANS	3.0	1.5	4.5	74.5
	−10.0	−5.0	−15.0	−85.0
NET ASSETS	29.0	14.5	99.0	29.0
CAPITAL AND RESERVES				
CALLED UP SHARE CAPITAL	10.0	5.0	17.0	10.0
SHARE PREMIUM ACCOUNT	4.0	2.0	67.0	4.0
PROFIT AND LOSS ACCOUNT	15.0	7.5	15.0	15.0
SHAREHOLDERS' FUNDS	29.0	14.5	99.0	29.0
Net tangible assets (£m)	29.0	14.5	43.5	−26.5
Total borrowings (£m)	17.0	8.5	25.5	95.5
Cash (£m)	5.0	2.5	7.5	7.5
Net borrowings (£m)	12.0	6.0	18.0	88.0
Gross gearing	58.6%	58.6%	25.8%	329.3%
Net gearing	41.4%	41.4%	18.2%	303.4%
Net gearing excluding intangibles	41.4%	41.4%	41.4%	Infinite
Shares in issue (millions)	20.0	10.0	34.0	20.0
Net asset value	145.0p	145.0p	291.2p	145.0p
Net tangible asset value	145.0p	145.0p	127.9p	−132.5p

Part II

Understanding the words

1

Additional information that you will find

There's more in a company's report and accounts than the main financial statements – in the case of public limited companies (plcs) a great deal more. Some of this is information required by company law (primarily, the **Companies Acts**). Some is information required by **accounting standards** and some is required under the rules for a **stock exchange listing**. And some information is designed to give the background to the items that appear in the **financial statements**. This information may often be vital to an understanding of the company's affairs.

The problem for an accounts user is in knowing where to look in the report and accounts for a particular item of information. This is because the rules which state what information must be provided do not necessarily say how or where it should be provided. An item that appears in one company's report and accounts within the **directors' report** might equally well be shown by another company in the notes to the accounts. You sometimes have to hunt round a little.

For this reason our guide categorises the additional information by topic rather than by location within the report and accounts. However, after each item we give an indication of where it is most likely to be found. Some topics that require more extensive explanation appear as separate items after this section.

Acquisitions

The directors are required to give details of significant acquisitions of other companies or businesses during the year, and acquisitions that are in train or have taken place since the year-end should be mentioned at least in **subsequent events** (q.v.). When you are studying a report and accounts it is important to establish right at the outset whether there have been major acquisitions or disposals during the year as this information will affect your interpretation of the figures in the profit and loss account and balance sheet. A large rise in pre-tax profits might be due not to improved performance but simply to the acquisition of another business whose figures have been incorporated for the first time. If pre-tax profits have risen sharply but earnings per share have not, you might look to see if the company had made an acquisition for shares during the year – or perhaps issued a lot of new shares in a rights issue (see page 64).

Activities

Principal activities of the company must be disclosed. This might be in the **directors' report**, but probably takes the form of a pointer to other sections like the **chairman's statement** and **chief executive's report** where the different business activities are discussed and analysed. A note to the accounts on **segmental information** should show the contributions from different parts of the business. (Directors' report, Notes to the accounts and elsewhere).

Associated companies and joint ventures

See **Investments**

Auditors

The **auditors' report** itself normally appears just before or just after the main financial statements (see separate section on pages 123–4). But there will be several other items relating to the auditors. A resolution to reappoint the auditors (or to appoint a different firm) will be listed as part of the business of the annual general meeting, as will a resolution to empower the directors to determine the remuneration of the auditors. The fee for the past year's audit will be shown in the notes to the accounts as one of the deductions made before arriving at the operating profit. And if the accountancy firm that undertook the audit also did other work for the company (tax planning and advice, perhaps) the amount it was paid for this additional work should be disclosed. This is sometimes a contentious issue, highlighted in the aftermath of the collapse of energy group Enron. Many commentators ask whether an accounting firm can be relied on to produce an independent audit if it is heavily reliant on the company for other types of work and thus keen to avoid argument or confrontation. (Notes to the accounts, Notice of meeting – see pages 129–30.)

Borrowed money

See **Creditors**

Capital commitments

At the end of a company's financial year it may have committed itself to expenditure on fixed assets (**capital expenditure**) that has not yet taken place. New plant and equipment may have been ordered that has not yet been delivered or paid for. Companies therefore provide a figure for the expenditure they had contracted for (were committed to) at the year-end. They may also show additional expenditure that had been authorised by the directors at that date, though firm contracts had not yet been entered into. These figures can be useful in drawing attention to a particularly heavy capital expenditure programme, with the attendant question of where the money is coming from, though a good finance director's report should address these issues anyway. (Notes to the accounts.)

Committees of the board

See separate section **The board of directors** on pages 111–12.

Contingent liabilities

Always check to see if a company includes a note to the accounts referring to contingent liabilities. These are liabilities which are not firm enough to be shown as such on the balance sheet, but which might translate into real liabilities at some point in the future. A typical example might be where the company is being sued for a large amount of money by a disgruntled customer. The company claims that it has a watertight defence against the claim and that no liability is expected to arise. But if it is wrong and the case goes against the company, the liability could become a real one. Another common example is where a company provides guarantees for loans taken out by its associated companies. If these associated companies get into financial trouble, the company could find itself responsible for repaying their loans under the guarantee. In very rare cases there is a contingent liability so large that it could threaten the company's continued existence if it translates into a real liability. Remember, you would have no inkling of this from looking at the balance sheet alone. (Notes to the accounts.)

Creditors

The notes to the accounts will give quite a lot of detail on the company's creditors, broken down between those due within one year (short-term liabilities) and those due after one year (medium- and long-term liabilities).

One of the main items in the short-term liabilities is likely to be the company's **trade creditors**, who are usually mainly suppliers who have not yet been paid. If there has been a major movement in this item over the year, you would want to know the reason. A large increase could be explained simply by a takeover during the year, with the creditors of the acquired company included in the figure for the group for the first time. Or it could be that the company's level of business, as reflected in its turnover figure, increased significantly during the year. In this case it would probably have bought more goods from suppliers and there would therefore have been larger amounts owing to suppliers on any given date (see page 84).

Money owing to suppliers is effectively an interest-free loan from the suppliers to the company. It is therefore a useful source of finance. But the position would look different if you suspected the trade creditors figure had increased because the company *was unable* to pay its suppliers. Or if the figure had reduced because suppliers had become doubtful about the company's financial health and had begun to insist on earlier payment.

The other major item under creditors, in the case of many companies, will be the money they have borrowed in one form or another. In fact, this information may be given in a separate note headed 'Borrowings', 'Loans' or something similar. Quite a detailed breakdown should be provided, and there is important information here.

First, there is the total amount of borrowed money. As we saw on page 26, this can be used to produce a **gearing ratio**, showing the balance between shareholders' money and borrowed money used in the business. This is an important measure of the financial health of the company.

Second, there is the **maturity** of the debt when the borrowed money has to be repaid. Overdrafts are technically repayable on demand and therefore have to be shown under **short-term liabilities**. Any other loans, or parts of loans, that are due for repayment within a year will also appear here. The longer-term loans will appear as **creditors that are due after one year** and they should be broken down according to repayment date. This is valuable information. Is a major loan repayable in a couple of years? Where will the cash come from to repay it? Will the company be able to replace it with a new loan on equal or better terms? A good **finance director's report** may address such issues and either there or here in the note to the accounts you may find references to **loan facilities**. This is money that the company has lined up to meet possible future needs but which it has not borrowed at this point.

Third, the breakdown should give information on which loans are **secured** and which are **unsecured**.

Fourth, the breakdown should distinguish between simple loans to the company and securities issued by the company to borrow money. Bonds that the company has issued are securities, will usually pay a fixed rate of interest and may go under a variety of different names; **debenture stock** is common. **Convertible bonds** are also securities that will appear here, with details of the conversion terms.

Fifth comes the **interest rate** on the debt. Where a company has many individual loans it may not give the interest rate on each but it should at least break the loans down between those at fixed rates of interest and those at floating rates, and provide details of the average interest rates that it pays. There is quite a lot you can infer from this detail. If the company's debt is mainly fixed-rate, the interest rate is reasonably low and the debt has some years to run before it is repaid, the company's finances are probably reasonably secure. It is not going to face higher finance costs if interest rates in the economy move sharply up in the next year or so. On the other hand, if it has long-term fixed-rate debt at a rate of interest that is high by today's standards, then you know that it is saddled with above-average finance costs for some time into the future. If the debt is mainly at floating rates of interest the company could be vulnerable to a general rise in interest rates in the economy. The additional interest it will have to pay could dent its future profits. On the other hand, it will get the benefit from any fall in general interest rates.

Sixth, there is the **currency** in which the money is borrowed. Large international companies in particular may have borrowings in many currencies. There are various reasons for this. A company with a large operation in America, say, might borrow in US dollars so that it matches the currency of its liability with the assets that it holds in that country. But a company might also borrow in an overseas currency simply because the interest rate was lower at the time than it would have been on a sterling loan in Britain. This has its dangers. If the value of the overseas currency subsequently rises against the pound sterling, then the loan will eventually cost more to repay in terms of sterling and any interest saving may have been more than wiped out.

Finally, be a bit careful when looking at the individual borrowings as the company may have used various **hedging** techniques to reduce its interest rate or currency risk. For example, it might have raised a loan in US dollars but **swapped** the proceeds into sterling. Or it might have borrowed floating-rate money but **swapped** it into fixed rate. There are various other forms of 'insurance' it might have used, such as **caps** or **collars**, to reduce its exposure to rising interest rates. The effect of **financial instruments** (q.v.) such as these should be explained, but the explanations are not always as clear as they might be. However, a good finance director's report will comment on the company's hedging policy and the instruments that it uses. (Notes to the accounts, Finance director's report.)

Debtors

These are the counterpart of creditors and the biggest item is likely to be trade debtors. This represents money that is owed to the company for goods or services that it has supplied to customers who have not yet paid. It is thus like an interest-free loan that the company makes to its customers. If a company allows its customers to delay too long before paying, it ties up its own cash resources and incurs higher interest costs. A big jump in debtors might reflect a takeover, a big increase in the level of business or simply that the company has become lax in chasing the money that is owed to it (poor cash management – see pages 84–5.)

Derivatives

See **Financial instruments**

Directors

See separate sections **The board of directors** (page 111) and **Pay and perks in the boardroom** (page 116).

Directors' interests in contracts

Where a company does business with one of its own directors or a business in which a director has a significant interest, this must be disclosed. This is to highlight the potential for conflicts of interest or 'sweetheart' deals. A typical example might be where a non-executive director is a partner in a firm of surveyors that earns fees from undertaking the valuation of the company's properties. (Directors' report or Notes to the accounts.)

Dividends

Details of the interim and final dividends per share, including those paid or payable on the different classes of capital if the company has more than one, will be provided. Note that the figures will be for the dividends relating to the year's activities. The final dividend, though relating to the year in question and proposed before the annual report goes out, is probably not paid until after the agm and is therefore actually paid in the current financial year, not the one just ended. If you want to see the dividends actually paid during the year you will need to look at the cash flow statement (see page 36), which will generally show the previous year's final and the last year's interim. Companies sometimes offer their shareholders the option of taking their dividends in shares (a **scrip dividend** – see page 72) rather than cash, in which case the details may be shown here. (Notes to the accounts, Directors' report.)

Donations, political and charitable

Companies are required to state how much (if anything) they have donated to charities or to political organisations and, in the case of political organisations, to name the recipients. Shareholders do not normally vote directly on these donations and you'll find occasional criticism of company directors who buy themselves political knighthoods by making donations to political parties with their shareholders' money. (Directors' report.)

Earnings per share

We saw when looking at the profit and loss account that earnings per share figures may be produced in a number of different ways: official FRS 3 figures, diluted earnings or earnings adjusted to exclude one-off items (see pages 54–7). A note to the accounts should explain the calculations that produced the different figures. Note that earnings are calculated on the weighted average number of shares in issue during the year which is not necessarily the same as the year-end figure. You may see references to FRS 14, which is the accounting standard setting out how the average and diluted share capital should be calculated. (Notes to the accounts.)

Employee share ownership plans (ESOPs)

Where a company has an ESOP, the notes to the accounts should give details of it and of the value of the shares that it holds in the company. These will be shown as **own shares** in the group's balance sheet. For more detail see separate section **Employee share ownership plans – and their dangers** (page 119). (Notes to the accounts.)

Exceptional items

Where exceptional items crop up in the accounts you can expect to find a bit more explanation of how they arose. If significant, they will probably be mentioned in the chief executive's review or finance director's review but the notes to the accounts should in any case include a breakdown of the items. (Notes to the accounts.)

Financial instruments

This term usually covers different mechanisms the company uses, often involving the use of **derivative financial products** or **derivatives**, to manage its interest rate and currency risks. A **swap** might be used, for example, to convert the interest payable on a loan from a fixed rate to a floating rate of interest, or vice versa. Since the use of instruments of this kind can greatly change a company's risk profile it ought to be explained where the detail of borrowings is given or in the finance director's report. (Notes to the accounts, Finance director's report.)

Fixed assets

There may be separate notes dealing with **intangible assets** and **tangible assets**, where the group has both. Goodwill is the most common **intangible asset**. We saw how it arose in the course of a takeover on page 91. The note should show the goodwill at the start of the year and any additions or disposals of goodwill during the year. It will also show how much depreciation or amortisation had been provided by the start of the year (out of previous years' profits) and how much additional amortisation was provided during the year. This leads to the figure for goodwill shown in the accounts, which is of course net of the amortisation provided to date.

The note on **tangible fixed assets** will be a little more detailed. Assets will be broken down between plant, machinery, motor vehicles, etc., on the one hand and land and buildings on the other. Land and buildings (also see **land and property**) may in turn be broken down between freehold, long leasehold and short leasehold. The figures at the start of the year will be followed by additions and disposals during the year to arrive at an end-year figure, before depreciation. Then we see how much depreciation had been accumulated by the start of the year out of prior-year profits, and the amount of depreciation provided in the latest year. Deducting the total accumulated depreciation gives the figures at which the assets appear in the accounts, which may be described as **net book amounts**. The detail provides a handy overview of the amount of investment by the company in fixed assets, either by direct purchase or by taking over the companies that own them. There are a couple of points to note. If companies lease assets under **finance leases**, instead of owning them in a legal sense, these leased assets will be treated in the accounts much as if they were owned (see page 126). And note that while plant and equipment will normally appear at cost less depreciation, land and buildings will sometimes be shown at market values rather than cost (see also **Leases** and separate section **Check on the company's accounting policies** (page 125). (Notes to the accounts.)

Interest payable

Whereas the profit and loss account probably showed simply the net interest payable, the breakdown in the notes to the accounts will show interest payable less interest receivable. If the company has different types of debt, the interest payable should be broken down between interest on bank loans and overdrafts, interest on long-term debt, etc. If any interest was **capitalised** (treated as part of the cost of an asset rather than charged against the year's profit – see pages 155–6) this should be made clear. (Notes to the accounts.)

Investments

Investments may fall into a number of different categories, and the detail may be given in a single note or a number of notes. First, there is the investment by the parent company in its subsidiaries. Since this is shown simply as the book value of the shares in subsidiaries that are held by the parent company (or occasionally as the parent company's share of the subsidiaries' net assets), it is rarely of great interest.

Then there are investments held by the group in **associated companies** (related companies), which we looked at on pages 50–1. The amount of detail given about the associated companies varies a lot. The group's investment in its associates is shown as its proportionate share of their net assets, plus any loans that it has made to these companies (this is known, incidentally, as the **equity method of accounting**). The identities of the main associates, and the group's shareholding in them, will appear somewhere in the accounts but probably under a separate heading such as 'group companies', which will also give details of the subsidiary companies. Where interests in associated companies or joint ventures form a significant part of a group's total assets, more details of the assets and liabilities of these associates and ventures should be shown in the notes to the accounts.

There may be other investments, in companies which are not associates, or in securities such as government bonds, which are held simply as an alternative to cash. If these are not being held for the long term they will appear under current assets rather than fixed assets. Investments in listed securities must be shown separately.

There may also be a category of investment headed **own shares**. This probably arises because the company sponsors an **employee share ownership plan (esop)** or **trust (esot)** – see page 119 for an explanation). (Notes to the accounts).

Land and property, value of

We've seen elsewhere that companies may show their land and buildings at what they cost (less depreciation) or at revalued figures. Where such properties are shown at cost, the **Companies Acts** require the directors to tell shareholders if, in their opinion, the market value is substantially different from the book figures and, if it is, to quantify the difference if this is important to shareholders. In theory this should provide useful information for anyone studying the accounts to get an idea of the real value of the company's assets. In practice it is a requirement more honoured in the breach than the observance and directors frequently fail to draw attention to quite large differences between book values and current market values. It may be that they think they will make themselves more vulnerable to a takeover if they show what the assets are really worth. Where land and property is shown at valuation rather than depreciated cost, you should find details of when it was last valued, and by whom. A fully independent external valuation by a firm of chartered surveyors may carry more weight than a directors' valuation, though the directors would probably have taken professional advice. See also separate section **Recognised gains and losses** (page 128). (Directors' report, Notes to the accounts.)

Leases

A company provides certain information on its liabilities under **finance leases** and **operating leases**, where part of the plant and equipment it uses is leased rather than owned outright. The section **Check on the company's accounting policies** on pages 125–6 explains the situation in more detail. (Accounting policies, Notes to the accounts.)

Loans

See **Creditors**

Long-term incentive plans (LTIPs)

Where a company operates a long-term incentive plan or LTIP to reward its directors with free shares the details will normally be set out in the remuneration committee report. See the separate section **long-term incentive plans for directors** (page 118) for more detail.

Operating profit and expenses

There is a lot more information in the **notes to the accounts** on the costs incurred in arriving at the group's operating profit than you will find on the face of the profit and loss account. You will see the turnover figure, then a figure for **cost of sales** (materials costs, wages and the rest). Deducting cost of sales from turnover gives a gross profit figure. Then there are other expenses to be charged, which may be described as net operating expenses. These include **distribution costs** and **administration expenses**. Specific costs which need to be itemised include the depreciation charge for the tangible fixed assets (and the charge for depreciation or amortisation of goodwill, if applicable) and the fees paid to the auditors. As we saw earlier under **auditors**, companies are also required to state the fees they paid to their auditors for services other than the audit itself. (Notes to the accounts.)

Options

See **Share options**

Own shares

See **Employee share ownership plans**

Parent company and group

Companies which consist of a parent and one or more subsidiaries are required to produce both a **profit and loss account** and a **balance sheet** for the group (**consolidated accounts**) and the same financial statements for the parent company alone. In practice, companies normally invoke an exemption which relieves them of the need to publish a **parent company profit and loss account**, so only the consolidated figures are shown. In this case you will probably find a note saying how much of the group profit was dealt with in the accounts of the parent. But consolidated and parent company balance sheets will both be required, sometimes published as separate accounts and sometimes as a single page, giving both consolidated and parent company figures. Notes to the accounts will show both consolidated and parent company figures where appropriate. (Financial statements, Notes to the accounts.)

Pensions

Information on the pension schemes run by the company is important, particularly if there is a funding shortfall or, at the opposite extreme, the company is taking a contributions holiday. Details of the contributions made by the company to its pension scheme over the year should appear in the notes to the accounts, perhaps under staff costs (q.v.) with more detail on directors' pensions in the remuneration committee report. See separate section **Understanding company pension schemes** (pages 121–2) for more detail.

Provisions for liabilities and charges

Remember that the **provisions** item in the balance sheet covers liabilities that are expected to arise in the future (see pages 50–1). The general rule is that when a company becomes aware that a particular liability is going to arise in the future, and it can be reasonably accurately quantified, the company should provide for it out of its current profits even if the money may not have to be paid out for a year or so. Suppose that a company is planning to close down one division of its operations and reckons this will cost £10m in redundancy and other closure costs. It makes a £10m provision out of its profits to the provision for liabilities and charges. Then this provision gradually reduces as the money is actually paid out in redundancy and other costs. The note will show the provision at the start of the year, broken down into different categories, show any more provisions made from the profit and loss account during the year and provisions used up during the year, and arrive at the size of the outstanding provisions at the end of the year. There are probably some potential liabilities for which the company does not make provisions because it thinks that in practice they will not arise. For example, if a company were to sell all of the properties that it owns there might be a big capital gains tax bill. But if the company has no intention of selling its properties it will not make a provision against this liability. However, it should state the likely size of this hypothetical liability all the same (this could be valuable information for any predator planning to acquire the company and break it up, in which case the tax might have to be paid when properties were sold). (Notes to the accounts.)

Reconciliation of movements in shareholders' funds

This is usually found either in the notes to the accounts or as a supplementary **financial statement** after the profit and loss account, balance sheet and cash flow statement. It contains some of the same information as will be found in the note on **reserves** (see below), but its main function is to identify the factors that led to the increase or decrease in shareholders' funds over the year. In other words, it shows why the value (for accounting purposes) of the shareholders' interest in the company rose or fell. (Financial statements or Notes to the accounts.)

Register of charges

This is worth mentioning, though you won't actually find it in the report and accounts. Where a company borrows money (via an overdraft, loan, issue of a bond or whatever) it may give a **charge** over some or all of its assets as security for the lender. The loan then becomes a secured loan or borrowing. For somebody wanting to assess the creditworthiness of a company, it may be important to know which, if any, of its assets are already charged as security for other loans. For this reason, companies have to file with the **Registrar of Companies** – in a **register of charges** – the details of any charges that they have given over their assets and also keep a similar register at their own offices. The register may be inspected by members of the public via **Companies House**, or at the company's office, and it can provide useful information for anyone studying the company's affairs as to who the lenders to the company are. In the report and accounts, a good finance director's report may give some detail of which borrowings are secured and the breakdown of borrowings in the notes to the accounts should also provide this information. (Finance director's report, Notes to the accounts.)

Reserves

The note on reserves or **movement in reserves** can provide a useful reminder of major financial events during the year. The note probably sets out the different reserves at the start of the year, additions or deductions during the year, and the figures at the end of the year. The **profit and loss account reserve**, for example, will have been increased by retained profits (the amount of the year's profit that was ploughed back into the business rather than being distributed as dividends – see pages 24–5). Conversely, it will have been reduced if the company made losses during the year. **Share premium account** will have been increased by the premium on any new shares issued (new shares are likely to have been issued at a price above their par value). If the company had commissioned a revaluation of its properties during the year, any increase over the previous book values would have been added to the **revaluation reserve** (see below), and so on. This note needs to be seen in conjunction with the note on **reconciliation of movements in shareholders' funds**. (Notes to the accounts.)

Revaluation reserve

Where a company has revalued some of its assets (usually land and property) any surplus over the previous book figure will be accounted for in this reserve. The notes should show any additions to the reserve during the year, and how they arose, thus drawing attention to any revaluations that have taken place. Sometimes the figures will show a reduction in the reserve. This usually arises when properties that had been revalued are subsequently sold. The surplus is thus translated into a cash receipt and no longer figures in this reserve. But the figure could, of course, also drop if properties are valued again and are shown to be worth less than previously. (Notes to the accounts.)

Segmental information

Companies which have more than one activity are required to give a breakdown of their business by activity. The more conscientious ones will also provide a useful analysis by geographical region. This information can be helpful by providing a picture of the relative importance of different parts of the business and of the company's exposure to economic conditions in different countries. Since companies are reluctant to give away information that could be useful to their competitors, they will sometimes try to find arguments for keeping the breakdown to a minimum (Notes to the accounts, Chief executive's review.)

Share capital

You will find in the note to the accounts the details of the company's share capital, including a record of any shares issued during the year. This will show the **authorised share capital** (the maximum the company is currently entitled to issue under its constitution) as well as the amount actually in issue. The **issued capital**, which is what you will see in the balance sheet, is probably described as 'allotted and fully paid'. The figures will show numbers of shares and the **nominal value** of these shares – be careful not to confuse the two. For example, a company with an issued capital of 40,000,000 25p shares would have issued capital of £10m, since each pound of nominal capital represents four shares. If major issues of shares have been made during the year (a rights issue or an acquisition for shares, perhaps) this will probably have been referred to at various points in the report and accounts (the directors' report, chief executive's review, etc.) Even where the company has made no major issues of shares, small numbers of new shares may have been created when directors exercised share options or where shareholders were given the opportunity to take their dividend in shares rather than cash (a scrip dividend). If the share capital includes classes of shares with complex or unusual rights, these should be explained. (Notes to the accounts.)

Share options

As well as giving details of their present share capital, companies are required to give details of options over shares that could result in the creation of new shares in the future. This is explained in more detail in the section **How share options work** on page 117. (Notes to the accounts, Remuneration committee report.)

Share premium account

A note will give details of changes to the share premium account (see pages 24–5) over the year, showing how the premium on any new shares issued above their par value has gone to swell the total. (Notes to the accounts.)

Shareholdings in company

Companies are required to identify all shareholders who individually own 3% or more of their share capital and to give the size of the shareholding. The big insurance companies and pension funds crop up frequently here, but there may be other shareholdings that are less easy to identify, particularly if they are cloaked in nominee names. Some companies also provide a breakdown of their shareholders between institutions, overseas investors, private investors, etc. For details of disclosure of directors' shareholdings, see separate section **Pay and perks in the boardroom** on page 116. (Directors' report, Notes to the accounts or Shareholder information.)

Staff costs

You will find, probably in the notes to the accounts, information on the group's wage bill, including additional costs such as National Insurance contributions and pension costs. Detailed information on the remuneration of the directors may appear at this point, but it is more likely to crop up elsewhere as a separate item, either in the notes or in the **remuneration committee's report**. See also **Pay and perks in the boardroom** on page 116. (Notes to the accounts.)

Staff numbers

Companies are required to provide employee numbers and this information may be broken down to a greater or lesser extent between different parts of the business. However, the figures provided are normally the average figures for the year, so they will not necessarily highlight recent large staff cuts or recruiting drives. Where a group employs part-time workers it may give the full-time equivalents. Combined with the information on staff costs, this allows you to work out the average salary throughout the group. It can be an interesting exercise to compare the movement in average salaries with the movement in directors' pay over a given period. (Notes to the accounts, Directors' report.)

Stocks

The overall figure for stocks that was shown in the balance sheet (see pages 16–17) should be broken down between **raw materials**, **work in progress** and **finished goods**. Watch out if the finished goods category is rising disproportionately. Perhaps the company is having problems in selling all that it produces. Stocks are normally shown at the lower of cost and net realisable value. In other words they are shown at what they cost, unless the value has fallen below the cost level for one reason or another - perhaps because some items are now obsolescent. In the case of some specific types of company, such as housebuilders, large amounts of land may be included here under stocks rather than under fixed assets. This is because the land is a 'raw material' that such companies use in their business, rather than a long-term asset. A 'land bank' of building land might actually be worth quite a lot more than it cost, if it has been held for some years, and this may be referred to somewhere in the report and accounts. Equally, in the past housebuilding companies have occasionally been forced to write down by very large amounts the value of the building land that they owned, following a slump in the housebuilding market. (Notes to the accounts.)

Subsequent events

Though accounts themselves are drawn up to a specific date (the end of the company's financial year) and reflect the position on or up to that date, the **Companies Act** requires the directors to mention in the annual report significant events affecting the company or its subsidiaries that have taken place since the year-end. (Directors' report, Chairman's statement, etc.)

Subsidiary companies

At some point in the report and accounts – often at the end of the **notes to the accounts** – a company will give a list of its significant subsidiary companies and its percentage shareholdings in those that are not wholly owned. It will also show whether these are directly owned or owned through other subsidiary companies. In other words, the parent company Bloggins plc might wholly own a subsidiary company called Payola Properties Ltd, which in turn owns 80% of Schlenter Estates Ltd. Bloggins's interest in Schlenter is thus 80%, though it is not held directly. At the same spot the parent company may give details of its associated companies and joint ventures.

Taxation

The note to the accounts will show the detail behind the tax charge in the profit and loss account. In particular, it should show any tax adjustments in respect of earlier years and the breakdown of the tax charge between UK **corporation tax** and tax paid overseas. Where a company pays tax overseas at a rate as high as in the UK it is not normally taxed again in the UK on these profits (it receives **double taxation relief**). (Notes to the accounts.)

Transactions with related companies

Companies are meant to quantify the amount of their business (if any) that has been undertaken with related companies. If you noticed that the company's biggest customer was a joint venture in which it had a 50% interest, you might want some reassurance that the transactions were on an arm's length basis. (Notes to the accounts.)

Ultimate parent

Companies which are controlled by another company must disclose the identity of their ultimate parent (Company information or Directors' report.)

2

What the narrative pages contain

Faced with a company's report and accounts, more experienced users probably turn first to the financial statements and the notes to the accounts. They only turn later to the narrative sections of the document for additional explanation. Newcomers may find it easier to read the narrative sections first.

Different companies present this narrative material in different ways and give it different names. But the key elements – whatever they are called – are likely to be a **chairman's statement**, a **review of the year's operations**, a **financial review** and a **directors' report**.

The chairman's statement probably provides the most succinct overview of the company's operations over the past year, with brief comment on trading conditions and key figures. Major events such as acquisitions are also likely to be referred to, and there may be a pointer to how the company expects to perform in the current year. It can be a useful starting point.

The review of the year's operations is likely to be a lot longer and it takes a number of different forms and names. It may be described as **chief executive's review** or **operating review**. It is likely to go into far more detail about the trading performance of different parts of the company, probably showing the volume of business and the profits or losses that each major division contributed to the group's results for the year and explaining the main factors that affected performance. In some cases this section may include a separate review by the chief executive of each of the company's main operating divisions.

The financial review or **finance director's review** is the narrative section that varies most widely in quality. At its worst it is little more than a listing of the main figures that appear in the profit and loss account and balance sheet. At its best it explains these figures and puts them into context in terms that are clear and simple enough to give a layman a firm grasp of the company's finances and of major developments during the year. Indeed, a really good finance director's review can – if read in conjunction with the financial statements themselves – serve as a useful tutorial for anyone wanting to widen his understanding of company accounts. So important is the finance director's review that we look at it in more detail later (see pages 109–10).

At some point after these three statements, but before the accounts themselves, you are likely to come across the **directors' report**. This is a part of the report and accounts that has a far longer history than relatively recent innovations like the finance director's report. It exists because there is certain information that the directors are required by the Companies Acts to provide each year in relation to profits, dividends, main activities, issues of shares, election of directors and so on. But now that the report and accounts has become much more informative than in the past, a lot of this information is likely to be provided elsewhere in the document anyway. So the directors' report may do little more than point to other locations where the requisite information may be found. It does, however, probably contain various statements about environmental policies, staff involvement policies, policies for the employment of disabled people and the like, which larger companies are required to provide. Alternatively, these may be found on the corporate governance pages (see below). They rarely make exciting or informative reading. The directors' report is, however, worth a quick flick through in case you spot something you may have missed elsewhere.

One item which might have formed part of the directors' report in the past but is now likely to be in a section of its own is the details of the company's directors (see **The board of directors** section on pages 111–12).

Close to, or forming part of, the directors' report you are likely to find a **corporate governance** section, though it may go under a variety of names. This is the real growth area of recent years. Companies are nowadays meant to observe a code of conduct on the way they run themselves and this results in the generation of many reports on individual aspects of the code, which are pretty incomprehensible unless you know the background. For this reason we provide a fuller explanation in the section on **corporate governance** on pages 114–15, and in individual sections on **directors' pay** and the **going concern statement**.

Just before the main financial statements you are likely to find the **auditors' report** and a **statement of accounting policies** (we deal with these in separate sections later). And after the main financial statements come the very detailed and important **notes to the accounts** which give more detail and explanation of the figures that appear in the accounts themselves.

Following the notes, one complexity you may come across in the case of major British-based international companies, is an alternative set of accounts produced according to United States accounting rules. These are probably described as **US GAAP accounts** (the GAAP stands for **Generally Accepted Accounting Principles**). These will be perfectly recognisable to somebody who understands British accounts, though will differ in their treatment of certain major items – the differences are beyond the scope of this book.

Every company provides certain basic information about itself, such as the address of its registered office, the names and addresses of its auditors and its principal bankers, stockbrokers and solicitors. Most large companies farm out the management of their share register rather than keeping it at the registered office, and in this case the name and address of the registrars who look after the register will also be given. In addition to this basic information, many large companies also include a specific page of **shareholder information**, which may include a **financial timetable**. Together or separately, these sections are likely to give dates for important events such as publication of interim and preliminary results, dividend 'xd' and payment dates, date of annual general meeting, etc. There will be some information on historical share prices (needed for certain tax computations) and perhaps the name of a public relations person who deals with shareholder queries.

Towards the end of the report and accounts (though it sometimes comes earlier) a company includes a page of **summary financial information**. Also commonly described as a five-year record, it gives – as might be expected – a five-year run of the key figures from profit and loss account, balance sheet and cash flow statement. This can be very useful in setting the latest figures into context.

The last item in the report and accounts is likely to be the notice of the company's forthcoming **annual general meeting (agm)** with details of the resolutions to be put to the meeting. Less commonly, this is inserted as a separate document. It is, of course, an invitation to the ordinary shareholders to exercise their right to attend the meeting but a **proxy card** will also be included to enable those who do not attend to cast their votes (this is explained in more detail in the section on **annual general meetings** on pages 129–30).

3

How a good financial review dispels the fog

A good **finance director's review** or **financial review** provides a bridge between the description of the year's trading in the chief executive's review and the cold figures that you find in the profit and loss account, balance sheet and cash flow statement. It shows how the company's operations during the year impacted on its finances and demonstrates the interaction between the main financial statements. As we suggested earlier, a really good finance director's report can be a useful learning aid for those trying to get to grips with company accounts.

You would, of course, expect to find a commentary on the main figures from the **profit and loss account** with explanations of significant changes. Let's take as an example a British company with international operations whose turnover has fallen over the past year though **operating profits** have risen. The finance director might explain that this was a result of the sale early in the company's financial year of a loss-making American subsidiary. The turnover of this American company is therefore no longer included in group figures since the sale. But with the losses out of the way, **profit margins** have improved across the group as a whole. **Earnings** have been helped by a reduction in the percentage **tax charge**. This is because the tax charge had been unusually high the previous year, since the company was not receiving relief against the tax on UK profits for the losses in America. With experience, you might be able to deduce points of this kind from information contained elsewhere in the report and accounts. But it saves a lot of time to have it clearly explained.

The **consolidated balance sheet** is, of course, the main source of information on the group's financial health and the finance director should talk you through it. The figures have, perhaps, shrunk somewhat from the previous year now that the figures for the former American subsidiary are no longer included. This has resulted in a reduction in the total for **fixed assets**, but also in the figures for **stocks**, **debtors** and **trade** and **other creditors** (both the trade creditors and the borrowings of the American company no longer appear). The American company was, say, sold for a cash sum that exceeded the value of its **net assets**. This has contributed to a modest increase in the group's **net assets per share**, the finance director explains.

He points out that the cash received from the sale of the American company has led to some increase in the group's **holdings of cash**. But he explains that the bulk of the money received was used to repay expensive (in terms of interest charges) **short-term borrowings**. The overall **gearing** of the group (net borrowings as a percentage of shareholders' funds) has decreased significantly as a result. There was also a benefit to the profit and loss account from reduced **interest charges** following the repayment of borrowings.

The finance director should also discuss the company's cash generation and cash outlays during the year, as set out in the **cash flow statement**, and their effect on the group's cash holdings and borrowings. This is a view from another angle of events that have already been touched on. In our example, apart from the group's normal cash generation from its operations, there will, perhaps, have been a small outflow as the cash held by the former American subsidiary is removed from the picture, but a big inflow in the shape of cash received from the sale. You would expect some comment on whether the company was generating enough cash to cover its **capital investment plans** or whether more will need to be raised from outside. Any capital-raising operations during the year (and the repayment of borrowings) should be analysed.

You would expect the finance director to provide a detailed analysis of the group's **borrowings**, or at least to talk you through the information provided in the notes to the accounts. This would probably cover how long the borrowings have to run, with details of average interest rates paid. This section should also look ahead, quantifying the group's likely future cash needs and mentioning what borrowing facilities for future use are already in place.

In addition to the explanation of the main financial statements, you would expect some discussion of the group's **hedging** policies. Hedges are a kind of insurance taken out against adverse movements in interest rates or exchange rates and may take the form of financial instruments such as **caps**, **swaps** or **forward rate agreements**. These can be highly technical and complex, but a good finance director's report should provide a reasonably simple explanation (perhaps in a separate section on **treasury policies**) of the group's approach towards protecting itself against interest rate and exchange rate risks, and the effect of the measures that it has taken.

4

The board of directors

While the **shareholders** – who are the **owners** – ultimately control a company and may vote to appoint or dismiss directors, it is the **directors** who are responsible for running the company day-to-day and year-to-year on behalf of the owners. The report and accounts normally gives quite a lot of information on the directors, including photographs and potted biographies. While the structure of the **board of directors** varies a certain amount from company to company, there are some common features.

First, the board of listed companies divides between **executive directors** and **non-executive directors**. Executive directors are employees of the company as well as directors, and they are responsible for running the business. As employees they draw a salary as well as a variety of other payments and perks. Non-executive directors, on the other hand, are directors without being employees. They are generally chosen for the business experience or expertise in specific areas that they can bring to the company. The amount of work they do for the company varies. It may be confined to attending board meetings, perhaps once a month. They may also serve on one or more of the committees of the board. While the non-executives do not run the company day-to-day, they can – in theory at least – act as a check on the actions of the executives who do run it and, if changes in management are clearly needed, the pressure might come from the non-executives. Non-executive directors do not receive a salary but are paid directors' fees for their contribution. Some non-executives are further qualified as **independent non-executive directors**. This status is easier to define by what it isn't than by what it is. For example, a former managing director who remains on the board as a non-executive director after his retirement would be unlikely to qualify as independent.

The most senior of the executive directors is the **chief executive** (**chief executive officer** or **CEO** in the increasingly popular American terminology), who may also be referred to as the **managing director**. Some companies have a chief executive or group chief executive, with a managing director immediately below him in the hierarchy. The chief executive is ultimately responsible for running the business and his is the name most likely to be associated with the company in press comment and elsewhere.

Next to the managing director or chief executive, the **finance director** (sometimes referred to as **chief financial officer** or **CFO**) is normally seen as the most important director. He takes overall responsibility for the company's financial strategy, though below him there is probably a **treasurer** (often not a director) who deals with the more nitty-gritty business of planning and managing cash and currency flows. There may be various other executive directors with specific responsibilities, such as marketing director, production director or research director. Or the other executives may each be responsible for running a specific division of the company.

The **chairman** of the company may be an executive or a non-executive director, though it is generally considered questionable policy nowadays to combine the offices of chairman and chief executive in a single person, because each should be able to act as a check on the other. The chairman is responsible for running the board of directors and will normally have a casting vote in the case of stalemate in board meetings, whereas the chief executive is responsible for running the business. The relationship between chairman and chief executive varies greatly from one company to another and there are some where the chairman rather than the chief executive will be viewed as the dominant figure.

Every company also needs a **company secretary** who may or may not be a director. The secretary is responsible for the administration of the company as a legal entity, and it is his name you will see at the bottom of the notice of the annual general meeting and similar documents. The details of the directors will also note their membership of various **committees of the board**, which consist mainly or wholly of non-executives – these committees are explained in the section on **corporate governance** (pages 114–15).

Each director, whether executive or non-executive, normally resigns from the board every three years **by rotation** and offers himself for re-election at the annual general meeting (unless he really wants to go, of course). The idea is to overcome the forces of inertia and, by giving shareholders a say at regular intervals, make it less easy for boards to become self-perpetuating bodies. New directors may be appointed in the course of a year, but their appointment then has to be ratified by a vote of shareholders at the next annual general meeting.

5

The directors' report and the legal requirements

The **directors' report** used to be the place where much of the legally required information on the company and its activities over the year was to be found. It still is, in the case of many smaller private companies. But large listed companies nowadays include information in so many different sections of the report and accounts – **chairman's statement**, **operating review**, **financial review**, **notes to the accounts** and so on – that the directors' report has generally declined in importance. It can still sometimes provide a concise and useful summary, however, or may point to where information is to be found elsewhere in the report and accounts. And if there is an item of information that you cannot put your hands on, always look in the directors' report, where it may well be tucked away.

The information that the directors of a company are required by law to provide is set out in the Companies Acts of which the last comprehensive revision was the **Companies Act 1985**. In the new millennium a comprehensive re-examination of company law was in train.

In the section of this book **Additional information that you will find** (page 95) are set out many of the items of information that a company is required to provide. These include many of the items on which the directors are required by the Companies Acts to report.

6

What corporate governance is all about

Whether or not it is in a separate section headed **corporate governance**, you'll find frequent references to aspects of governance in the report and accounts of a listed company. Though it may occupy many pages, much of it is totally incomprehensible unless you know the background. The word 'governance' itself doesn't help – you don't come across it often except in this context. The sense in which it is used is to describe the way in which the company is steered and regulated from the very top – by the board of directors – and the way in which this top governing body administers and regulates itself.

It all started in the early 1990s with a perception that the running of companies – in an administrative and financial sense – was in need of improvement. There were insufficient checks and balances at board level to prevent abuses and questionable practices. A committee, the **Cadbury Committee**, examined the issue and – in traditional British fashion – came up with a code of practice generally known as the **Cadbury Code**. Its main thrust was towards greater disclosure and certain measures to put executive directors under greater scrutiny, eliminate boardroom abuses and improve the direction of the company.

The original Code was later reviewed and amended by other committees, one of which – the **Greenbury Committee** – dealt specifically with issues of **directors' remuneration** (a suitably weighty term for 'pay and perks'). In the mid-1990s, rocketing **boardroom salaries** and benefits were inviting much press comment and causing some embarrassment to the government.

The efforts of these various committees culminated in a document known as the **Combined Code**, which is the one that companies are meant to observe today. The Combined Code is now attached to the **Listing Agreement**, the document that sets out the rules that companies must follow if they want their shares listed on the stock exchange. Again, this works in a typically British way. Companies are not forced by the stock exchange or the **Financial Services Authority** (Britain's **financial regulator**, which now administers the Listing Agreement) to follow every recommendation of the Combined Code but they must set out in their report and accounts the extent to which they conform to it, and must disclose and justify any departures from what the Code considers to be best practice.

What areas does the Code cover? One of its main thrusts is the role of **non-executive directors**. Some countries (Germany, for instance) have two-tier boards, with a Supervisory Board of non-executives overseeing the Management Board of executive directors who run the company. British companies have a single or **unitary board**. But within this single board the non-executive directors, in addition to their other functions, are exhorted to exercise a supervisory role over the executive directors. In part they do this through various committees that the Code recommends. The Code stipulates that non-executive directors should make up at least a third of the board and that a majority of them should be independent of management and free from other interests that could prevent their exercising independent judgement. The main committees on which all or some of them will sit are:

*   Remuneration committee
    The **remuneration committee** is meant to set boardroom pay policy and determine the pay and perks of individual executive directors. It should consist entirely of independent non-executive directors. The idea is to prevent the executives from setting their own pay and in the annual report the remuneration committee is meant to set out the company's remuneration policy for its directors. The pay and perks of each individual director should also be disclosed (see section **Pay and perks in the boardroom** on page 116 for more detail).

- Audit committee

  The **audit committee** should be composed entirely of non-executive directors, of whom a majority should be independent (see section on **the board of directors**). The functions of the audit committee may vary, but it should review the company's internal control procedures – in effect, conducting a form of internal audit. It would also review the scope and results of the external audit and monitor the independence of the external auditors. If the external auditors and the executive directors enjoy too cosy a relationship, the audit committee should – in theory at least – be able to spot it.

- Nomination committee

  With a majority of non-executive directors, the **nomination committee** should make recommendations to the board as a whole on new board appointments. This should help to achieve board balance and prevent the executives from simply recruiting supporters or cronies when vacancies occur.

In addition to recommending committees of the board for specific purposes, the Code has a number of other recommendations relating to directors. It considers that there are two separate jobs at the top of the company: responsibility for running the board and executive responsibility for running the company's business. No one person should have 'unfettered powers of decision'. This is why the **chairman** and the **chief executive officer** should normally be different people. If one person combines the two roles, the company will have to justify it.

It is also recommended that all directors should be subject to **election** by shareholders and each should submit himself for re-election at least every three years. Directors' **service contracts** should not run for more than a year. Where they do (and they often do) this should be noted and justified in the annual report. One of the ideas behind this is to prevent directors claiming massive payments by way of **golden handshakes** if they are ousted before their contract expires – the longer the director's contract has to run, the bigger the **compensation payment** that can normally be claimed.

One other significant item that is normally included under the 'corporate governance' heading in the report and accounts is the **going concern statement**. Since this requires a bit of technical explanation, we have given it a section to itself (see page 120).

7

Pay and perks in the boardroom

Enormous amounts of space are taken up in the report and accounts nowadays by the **remuneration committee's report** on **boardroom pay policies** and by the details of the **pay and perks** of each director. It is odd that this should be necessary and it is perhaps a measure of the extremely complex ways in which directors reward themselves. In a large company a director might receive:

- a **basic salary**
- an **annual bonus** of up to 50% of salary, supposedly geared to some measure of the company's performance
- **share options** and/or
- shares awarded under a **long-term incentive plan (LTIP)**
- **benefits in kind** such as car, life assurance, etc.
- generous **pension provision**.

It is the job of the remuneration committee of **independent non-executive directors** to set the salaries and benefits for the executive directors. In doing so they usually call heavily on the services of **remuneration consultants**, specialist firms that monitor and advise on executive pay. So the remuneration committee report will generally say that the committee sets pay and perks at a level that will attract and retain suitable executive talent, and in doing this it has looked at pay levels for comparable jobs in other companies, etc. In practice, it would be a bold committee of non-executives that told the executive directors that they did not deserve at least the average paid by other companies. Thus, if every executive is brought up at least to the average for the job, that average can only increase by leaps and bounds. Remuneration committees were originally introduced to prevent the executives from setting their own pay and to act as a brake on spiralling boardroom pay and perks. In practice, the rate of increase in directors' pay may well have accelerated since remuneration committees were introduced.

You will find a table, probably in the remuneration committee's report but it could be in the notes to the accounts, setting out the pay, bonuses and benefits in kind received by each director for the year. Details of share options that they hold or shares granted under an LTIP are probably shown in a separate table (see pages 117 and 118 for descriptions of how these work). Companies are discouraged by corporate governance guidelines from offering both share options and LTIP benefits to the same directors, though many do. You will also find a note of directors' existing shareholdings in the company (this is required information) though these could well be shares that they bought with their own money.

The **pension benefits** the director acquired during the year are also likely to be shown separately. This is a complex issue. What is important is not so much the contribution to the pension scheme made on behalf of the director in question that year, but the amount by which his pension entitlement increased. If his basic salary went up from £300,000 to £500,000 and he would be entitled on retirement to a pension of two-thirds of salary, the salary increase would have raised his prospective pension from £200,000 a year to £333,333. Thus, the potential benefit has increased by £133,333 over the year even though the contribution paid into the scheme for that director during the year might have been only £20,000. In practice, the calculations are a little more complex than illustrated here, but our figures serve to demonstrate the principle. There is, however, a limit on the size of pension that can be paid by a tax-approved pension scheme. Since directors' entitlements often exceed this limit you will probably find details of various top-up arrangements made on behalf of directors to ensure that they get their full whack.

8

How share options work

One of the favourite ways for companies to give their directors extra rewards and an incentive towards greater performance has long been the grant of **share options**. Though share option schemes have given way in many companies to **long-term incentive plans** or **LTIPs** (see page 118), the **executive share option scheme** is still very common. Where a company runs such a scheme, you will find it referred to in the annual report and accounts, probably in the **remuneration committee** report. You will also find details of the number of options granted to each director and of options exercised during the past year. To understand this detail, you need to know how share options work.

The basic principle is simple. The company grants options over, say, 100,000 shares to one of its directors at the share price ruling at the time of grant. Let's say the company's shares were quoted at 300p at the time. What this means in practice is that the director has the right to buy 100,000 shares in the company at a price of 300p (this is the **exercise price**), probably at any time within ten years, except that he cannot usually exercise this right in the first three years after the grant. When the director decides to exercise his option, the company normally creates the new shares which are sold to the director at 300p each.

So suppose that the company performs well, its profits and dividends rise, and that five years after the options were originally granted the share price on the stock market has risen to 550p. Our director now decides to **exercise** his right to buy for 300p shares which he can immediately sell in the market at 550p, or a profit of 250p per share. If he decides to exercise his options over all 100,000 shares at this point, the company creates the necessary 100,000 new shares, our director pays £300,000 for them and probably immediately sells them for £550,000. He thus walks away with a profit of £250,000 subject to whatever tax may be due.

Share option schemes have come in for criticism because they do not always reward performance. The company's share price might be carried up by a raging bull market on the stock exchange, even though the company itself had not performed particularly well. For this reason a **performance criterion** may also be built in, though it is rarely demanding. For example, the scheme may stipulate that the options may be exercised only if the company's earnings per share have exceeded the rate of inflation by, say, two percentage points a year over a given period.

You will find details of the options held by each director at the start of the company's year, any further options granted during the year or existing options exercised, and the number held at the end of the year. For each grant of options you will see the exercise price and the earliest and latest dates at which they may be exercised. The company also states its share price at the end of the year and the range within which the share price moved during the year. This detail is normally provided in the remuneration committee report or as a note to the accounts. With a bit of detective work you can deduce roughly the profits made by directors on exercise of options and the inbuilt profit that remains stored up for the future.

Shareholders would normally need to vote to approve the establishment of a new share option scheme because it involves the issue of shares by the company in the future. However, there is one type of option that requires no creation of shares. This is the so-called **phantom option**. Suppose our company grants phantom options rather than real options on 100,000 shares at 300p and again the share price has risen to 550p after five years. If our director decides to 'exercise' his phantom options at this point, the company does not sell him any shares but simply hands over as a bonus the £250,000 profit he would have made had he held real options.

9

Long-term incentive plans for directors

Long-term incentive plans or **LTIPs** were introduced by many larger companies to replace or supplement share option schemes (see page 117) as a way of spurring their directors and senior executives to greater performance. Or that is the theory! Shareholders are meant to vote to approve the establishment of a new LTIP and, if the company runs such a scheme, you should find the details in the annual report and accounts, probably in the **remuneration committee's report**. The LTIP is meant to be superior to share options in that it rewards performance over a longer period (though in practice usually only three years) and does not pay out just because of a bull market on the stock exchange.

LTIPs take many different forms, but a common pattern is as follows. Each director is given a **provisional grant** of a certain number of free shares: let's say 100,000 shares. But he does not receive these shares at the time. Instead, the company's **performance** is measured over the next three years. A popular **measure of performance** is **total shareholder return** or **TSR**. This is a combination of the dividends paid and the gain or loss arising from the movement in the share price over the period.

At the end of the three years the company compares the total shareholder return that it delivered with the TSR achieved by other comparable companies. If our company is a member of the 'Footsie' index of 100 leading companies, it might compare itself with the other 99 Footsie members. If its TSR is among the 25 highest achieved by this group, then each director might receive outright all 100,000 shares that had been provisionally awarded. If our company's position in terms of TSR was somewhere between 74 and 50, the directors might receive only a pro-rata proportion of the shares, and the remainder would be lost. If the company was in the bottom half by performance, the chances are they would lose all the provisionally gifted shares.

With an LTIP, the free shares awarded to the directors are often not new shares created by the company but existing shares that have been bought in the open market by an **employee share ownership plan** or **ESOP** sponsored by the company (see page 119 for more about ESOPs).

10

Employee share ownership plans – and their dangers

A lot of larger companies operate **employee share ownership plans** or **trusts** (**ESOPs** or **ESOTs**). These trusts buy the company's own shares in the stock market with the help of financial donations from the company, loans from the company or bank loans guaranteed by the company. The idea is usually that these shares are then available as part of a **bonus** or **incentive plan** for employees. In practice this usually means the directors and senior executives. An ESOP is often used to supply the free shares that are awarded under a **long-term incentive plan** or **LTIP**.

In theory an ESOP is a trust, managed by a trustee, and independent of the company. But the company is generally at risk if the shares held by the ESOP fall in value, because the company provided or guaranteed the loans used to buy them. For this reason the accounting authorities insist nowadays that in most cases the shares held by the ESOP should be treated in the accounts as if they were owned by the company. This is the reason you will often find a heading for **own shares** among a company's assets. The notes to the accounts should give more detail about the ESOP, including the current value of the shares that it holds. Incidentally, it may be a cause for concern if you come across an ESOP that has very large amounts tied up in shareholdings in the company. If the company runs into trading difficulties, its share price is likely to drop. This reduces the value of the 'own shares' on the balance sheet, which reduces the company's asset value, which could spark off a further fall in its shares. A number of companies have seen their problems compounded in this way.

Why a 'going concern' statement is needed

The accounts of a company are normally prepared on a **going concern basis**. In other words, the assumption is that the company is viable and will continue in business. This is important. If the company is not a going concern, the accounts would need to be prepared on a very different basis. So shareholders and creditors need to be very worried indeed if the **auditors** state in their report that they have doubts as to whether the company is a going concern. A statement that the auditors 'assume continuing support from the company's bankers' probably also casts some doubt on the company's future. They would not mention this unless they felt that the company would be in bad trouble without this support, and that there is some doubt whether the company can continue to deserve it.

Whereas accounts prepared on an **historical cost basis** are appropriate for a going concern, a different form of accounts would be needed if the company is to be **wound up** or **liquidated**. In this situation the important issue is not so much what the assets cost but what they will fetch if they have to be sold (particularly if they have to be sold in a hurry). And there will be sale costs to meet as well. So accounts prepared on a **liquidation basis** are likely to come up with much lower figures for the assets than you would find in normal historical cost accounts.

It is a reasonable assumption that most companies that are listed on the stock exchange are going concerns. But perhaps directors sometimes make this assumption a bit too readily and should be forced to question it. This is the idea behind obliging them to produce a formal statement saying that, to the best of their knowledge, the company is a going concern. It makes them look forward a bit and ensure, among other things, that the company has sufficient finance lined up for its needs. The directors should be (and almost certainly are) doing this anyway. But it's no bad thing if they have to put their name to it.

Understanding company pension schemes

Most larger companies run **pension schemes** for their employees – including the executive directors. In Britain – unlike some other countries – these are normally **funded pension schemes**. This means that the company does not simply pay pensions to former employees each year out of its profits. Instead, each year that the employee works for the company, it sets aside a certain amount of money. The money is probably provided partly by the company and partly by the employee. This money is invested in a **fund** that is separate from the finances of the company itself and the fund builds up to provide the pensions at the end of the day. Thus, in theory at least, the money for the pensions is still there, even if the company itself later goes bust.

Within this pattern there are two different types of scheme. With one, the employee is promised a pension at retirement age that will be a certain proportion of the salary he was earning when he retired. This is known as a **final salary scheme** or a **defined benefit scheme**. A good scheme might provide, say, a maximum pension of two-thirds of final salary. Each year that the employee works for the company, up to a maximum of 40 years, he earns a pension entitlement of one-sixtieth of his final salary. Thus, if he works for the one company for 40 years he earns a pension of forty-sixtieths of his final salary, which is two-thirds. In practice, since employees change jobs, they may end up earning part of their eventual pension with one employer, part with another.

Unfortunately for employees, many companies are now winding down their final salary schemes or closing them to new entrants. This is partly because of the perceived risk to the employer and partly because of a change to the taxation treatment of dividends on investments, introduced by New Labour shortly after it came to office. An important third factor is the introduction of a new accounting standard: FRS 17 (see below).

The other main type of funded pension scheme is the **money purchase** or **defined contribution pension scheme**. Again, regular contributions are made for each employee, and the money is invested in a fund separate from the company's own finances, but the employee is not promised a pension that is a specific proportion of his salary. Instead, the pension he gets depends on the amount of money that has built up in the fund and the size of pension that this will buy when he reaches retirement age.

A final salary scheme often offers the most attractive benefits for the employee but carries the greatest risk for the company. The company does not know what its employees will be earning when they retire, perhaps 40 years off. It does not know in advance what returns will be earned on the money in the pension fund and how fast it will therefore build up. What happens in practice is that **actuaries** calculate the pensions the scheme is likely to have to provide and put a figure on this liability. They also calculate what returns are likely to be earned on the invested money: the assets of the scheme. From this they can work out what contributions need to be made each year so that the assets will match the liabilities and there will be enough money to pay the pensions. There is not a separate pot of money for each employee. The actuaries are looking at whether the scheme as a whole will be able to cover its likely liabilities to all members.

If investment returns turn out better than the actuaries had expected in a final salary scheme, the fund will build up faster than expected and may show a **surplus** when compared with the likely liabilities. In this case the company may try to take some of the surplus out of the scheme for its own use, or at least cease its contributions for a few years. Such a **contributions holiday** obviously boosts the company's profits; a significant cost has temporarily disappeared. On the other hand, if salaries rise faster than expected (increasing the pension fund's liabilities, since the pension entitlements will rise in line) or investment returns are lower than expected (decreasing the rate of growth of the assets) the scheme may show a **deficit**. The assets will not be sufficient to cover the liabilities and the company might have to make a top-up injection into the fund or at least step up the annual contributions to eliminate the deficit over a period of years. This is a risk that does not arise with the money purchase scheme, since no particular level of pension has been promised.

Companies running final salary schemes will have the scheme valued by actuaries every few years to identify surpluses or deficits and the possible need for remedial action. If a company sponsors a final salary scheme for its employees, you need to look at the detail. If the scheme is **underfunded**, this points to additional costs for the company in the years ahead. If the scheme is in surplus and the company is currently taking a contributions holiday, you need to remember that there will be an adverse effect on profits when it needs to start paying contributions again. The information is most likely to appear in the notes to the accounts, though it might appear elsewhere and there will probably be references to pensions in the **remuneration committee's report**.

The accounting for final salary pensions schemes is undergoing change as a result of a new accounting standard, **FRS 17**. Traditionally, the assets and liabilities of a pension fund were regarded as separate from those of the company itself and did not appear anywhere on the face of the company's main financial statements. The investments in the scheme were also valued not at market prices but via an actuarial process that smoothed out the effect of stock market peaks and troughs. However, once FRS 17 is fully in force, companies will – for accounting purposes – need to show on their own balance sheets the surplus or deficit on the pension schemes that they run. And the pension scheme's investments will have to be shown at market values. The effect will be that a pension scheme that appeared very well funded one year could easily show a significant deficit the next if the value of its investments had been reduced by a sharp fall on the stock exchange. And the companies' own finances will appear weaker as a result of this deficit appearing on the balance sheet. It is a risk that a number of companies are unwilling to run and is contributing to the winding down of final salary schemes.

13

What auditors do – and don't do

Auditors are independent firms of accountants who review a company's accounts and certain other information in the annual report. They then state whether, in their view, the accounts give a **true and fair view**. The accounts themselves are the responsibility of the company's directors, though they may consult the auditors in the course of preparing them. The auditors are effectively a safeguard for the **shareholders (members)** to whom their report is addressed. If the directors were trying to pull the wool over the eyes of the shareholders by misrepresenting the company's true position, then it would be up to the auditors to spot it. However, there is frequent debate – and particularly in the aftermath of the collapse of energy giant Enron – as to whether auditors should see their role as that of a watchdog or a bloodhound. In other words, should they simply be keeping a watchful eye on things or should they be sniffing actively for trouble?

Auditors are appointed and paid by the company, but shareholders are asked at the **annual general meeting (agm)** to approve their reappointment (or the appointment of a different firm) and to authorise the directors to fix their remuneration. If shareholders were not satisfied that the auditors were doing a good job, they could signal the need for change by voting against it.

The **auditors' report** usually appears in the annual report and accounts just before or just after the main financial statements. It should always be checked when you are looking at a company's report. Ninety-nine times out of a hundred it will give the accounts a clean bill of health. In the other 1% of cases it can give a vital warning of possible trouble.

The report follows a pretty standard pattern. It begins with a statement that the auditors have audited the accounts. Then there are normally three main headings:

* relative responsibilities of directors and auditors
* basis of audit opinion
* opinion.

The first of these sections makes it clear that the auditors are not responsible for preparing the accounts, only for reviewing them. It sets out the auditors' legal and other responsibilities and various areas that they will review. They will point out if the company has not kept proper records, has not prepared the accounts in accordance with the Companies Acts, has not provided the auditors with all the information that they required, and so on. Companies in Britain are required to prepare their accounts in accordance with **accounting standards** (these are now published by the **Accounting Standards Board**) and they must note and justify any departure from these standards. The auditors will also mention that they have looked at other information in the report and accounts to see whether it is consistent with the financial statements themselves. One particular item that they will single out is the company's statement on **corporate governance**, where the company will state whether it has observed the provisions of the **Combined Code** (see corporate governance section on page 114).

The 'basis of audit opinion' section will say that the auditors have followed the relevant auditing standards in carrying out their work, with a brief explanation of some of the factors involved. They will, for example, have carried out spot checks on the supporting evidence for figures in the accounts, they will have reviewed whether the assumptions made by the directors are reasonable, and so on.

With the 'opinion' section we come to the real meat. If all is well, the auditors will give an **unqualified opinion** saying that the accounts give a **true and fair view** of the state of affairs of the company and of the profit or loss for the year and have been prepared in accordance with the Companies Acts. It is where the auditors' opinion departs from this standard format that you need to take note. The most serious divergencies are where the accounts 'do not give a true and fair view' (an **adverse opinion**) or where the auditors are unable to form an opinion (a **disclaimer of opinion**). More common are the cases where there is something specific that the auditors are unhappy about, which they will describe in their report, though they are still prepared to say that the accounts give a true and fair view, subject to a reservation on this specific issue. This would be a **qualified opinion**. Perhaps they have disagreed with the directors on the treatment of a particular item in the accounts. Perhaps some accounting records were missing in a relatively minor subsidiary company. A qualified report should always sound warning bells and the circumstances will deserve a closer look. You will need to form your own view on whether the qualification throws serious doubts on the running of the company, or whether it relates to a relatively minor technical issue. An adverse opinion or a disclaimer of opinion is, of course, far more serious and sometimes has more in common with a death knell than a warning bell.

14

Check on the company's accounting policies

Companies normally take a couple of pages to set out the policies adopted in preparing the accounts. This statement of **accounting policies** is likely to appear just before or just after the main financial statements. A lot of it is generally routine, but there can be information that is important or helps in interpreting the accounts.

The first point to note is that companies are meant to say when there has been a **change in accounting policies** since the previous year (this may also be referred to in the notes to the accounts). There will generally be a perfectly good reason for such changes. The cases you need to look at closely are changes which may have allowed the company to present its results in a more favourable light. We will come back to this point below.

The statement probably kicks off by saying that the accounts have been prepared in accordance with applicable **accounting standards**, and under the **historical cost convention**. The reference to historical cost may be followed by a qualification like 'as modified by the revaluation of certain properties'. The accounting standards referred to are the **Financial Reporting Standards** or **FRSs**, which are issued by the **Accounting Standards Board** (a body that in effect has the backing of government). Different standards apply to different aspects of the accounts. Some earlier accounting standards, produced under a different regime, are also still in use. These are known as **Statements of Standard Accounting Practice** or **SSAPs**. Accounting standards are currently undergoing a period of change and within a few years all companies in the European Union – including British companies – whose shares are listed on one of its stock exchanges will be required to produce accounts according to international accounting standards. These are produced by a body called the **International Accounting Standards Board**.

The historical cost convention is the one used in most British accounts. It means that assets are generally stated at what they cost, less allowances for depreciation in the case of **fixed assets** and possible write-downs in the case of **current assets** if these are no longer worth as much as was paid for them (fixed assets must also be written down if they suffer a permanent fall in value). You will see that stocks are usually described as valued at the **lower of cost and net realisable value.** So the starting point for most figures for assets that appear in the accounts is cost, and the figures don't claim to tell you necessarily what these assets would now be worth. The exception is certain assets in which there is a ready market and which can be valued fairly easily – properties are the most common example. Companies have a choice of showing the properties they use in their business at cost or at updated **valuations**, though properties held as investments rather than for use are meant to be shown at revalued amounts. Where updated valuations are used, this is clearly a departure from the historical cost principle – hence the qualification we referred to above. For companies that own a lot of property it is important to know if the figures in the books are current values or outdated historical ones. In the latter case, the company's true assets might be considerably more valuable than appears from the accounts.

There will probably also be a note on the treatment of **goodwill**. This may point out that the treatment changed in 1998 when the applicable accounting standard changed, and goodwill acquired since that date is **capitalised** (shown as an asset) in the balance sheet. It is probably **amortised** (written down in value or **depreciated**) each year over its estimated life. But in some cases the company calculates that goodwill is holding or increasing its value, and it does not therefore provide amortisation (see page 89).

The note on **depreciation of tangible assets** can be important. Companies normally depreciate fixed assets over their estimated useful lives, often using the **straight line method**. You have, say, a machine which you think has a useful life of ten years and at the end of the ten years you think you might be able to sell it for £5,000 as scrap. You paid £105,000 for it, so you deduct from your profits each year the sum of £10,000 in depreciation to write down its value. By the end of the ten years its value in the accounts will thus have been written down to its **residual value** of £5,000. Now, if you reckoned instead that the machine had a useful life of 20 years, you would depreciate it over 20 years, which means that you only have to provide £5,000 out of your profits in each year. Your profits would thus be £5,000 higher. It is because companies can 'improve' their profits in this way that you need to look carefully at any change in depreciation policies.

The accounting policies section will probably also contain a note on the treatment of **leases**. Some companies choose to lease the assets they use rather than buying them outright. But there are different types of lease. If a company leases a major item of machinery (or even a whole plant), in practice it probably operates the asset much as if it owned it and is responsible for repairing and maintaining it. Indeed, it probably has the right to acquire it at the end of the lease. On the other hand, if a company leases a photocopier, it may well be that the supplier (the legal owner or lessor) remains responsible for repairing and maintaining the machine, so the position is not the same as if the company owned the photocopier outright. The chances are that the lease of the major item of machinery is treated as a **finance lease** whereas the lease of the photocopier is treated as an **operating lease**. The distinction is important because the accounting treatment is different.

Assets leased under a finance lease are treated in the accounts very much as if the company did, in fact, own the asset even though it is not the legal owner. The asset is included under the company's own fixed assets, the company provides depreciation for it, and the payments the company is committed to make to the lessor over the life of the lease are shown as a liability, much as if the company had borrowed the money to buy the asset. An asset held under an operating lease is not included in the company's own assets and does not therefore appear on its balance sheet. The company simply has to show, probably in a note to the accounts, the annual payments that it is committed to make under operating leases. There have been proposals to abolish the distinction between the different types of lease, which is sometimes exploited by companies, and treat virtually all leases much as if they were finance leases. This has not yet happened. Note that property leases are normally treated as operating leases. A company that is committed to paying large amounts of rent over, say, the next ten years does not therefore have to show this liability in its balance sheet.

For companies that buy or sell abroad, swings in **exchange rates** can make a big difference to the published figures, so you should also find a note on how the company deals with **foreign exchange**. A common pattern is to include a transaction at the exchange rate ruling at the date it took place. Assets or liabilities held overseas, however, are normally converted into sterling at the rate ruling on the last day of the financial year. If a company uses **financial instruments** such as **swaps** to protect it against currency swings you will probably find a brief explanation of how these are accounted for, though with any luck there should be a more comprehensive explanation in the finance director's report or in the notes to the accounts.

Another point to look out for is the company's treatment of pensions and the type of pension scheme that the company runs for its employees. An **underfunded pension scheme** could be a big future liability (see separate section on pensions on page 121).

15

Historical cost profits and losses

Companies are required to provide a **note of historical cost profits and losses** where these would differ significantly from the figures actually shown in the accounts. You will see that many companies simply state that there is no significant difference. The reason for this note is that some companies carry all their assets at **historical cost** whereas others may **revalue** certain assets, particularly properties. This could, in some circumstances, affect the published profit figures. In this case the note is needed so that the performance of companies with different accounting treatments can be compared on level terms.

Take an example. Historical Holdings plc has an office building that stands in its accounts at a depreciated cost figure of £10m. Ready Revaluers plc has an identical office building, bought at the same time for the same price. But it had the office block revalued last year and incorporated the new value of £15m into its accounts. Both companies then sell their office buildings, in each case for £16m. Historical Holdings shows a profit of £6m on the transaction in its accounts (the difference between the sale price and the figure at which the property stood in the accounts). Ready Revaluers shows a profit of only £1m on the identical transaction, since the property had already been written up to £15m in its accounts. In these circumstances Ready Revaluers' note of historical cost profits and losses would add back into its published profits the extra £5m profit that would have been shown had the office block been carried in the accounts at historical cost.

16

Recognised gains and losses

The **statement of total recognised gains and losses** draws attention to events during the year which may have affected the value of the company (in accounting terms) even though they did not feature in the **profit and loss account**.

The starting point is the year's profit as shown in the profit and loss account, after minority interests and preference dividends (if any) but before dividends on the ordinary shares. Suppose this figure comes to £100m. But suppose also that the company commissioned a **revaluation** of the properties that it owned during the year and that this disclosed a surplus of £30m over the **book figures**. The new revalued figure was written into the accounts. Now, if the company had sold properties for a profit of £30m, this would have appeared in its profit and loss account. But it did not sell them. It simply established that they were worth an extra £30m and included this extra value in its accounts. It was a gain in value that the company **recognised**, even though no transactions were involved. The revaluation increased shareholders' funds by £30m. This £30m would therefore be added in the statement of total recognised gains and losses to the £100m published profit figure to give total recognised gains of £130m for the year.

Other items which feature frequently in this statement are gains or losses on the value of assets (in sterling terms) resulting from movements in the value of foreign currencies relative to the pound sterling over the year. These may be described as 'currency translation differences'.

17

Annual general meetings and the voting procedures

A company is required to hold an **annual general meeting (agm)** each year. **Ordinary shareholders** may attend, ask questions and cast their **votes. Preference shareholders** do not normally have a vote unless their dividend has been **in arrears** for a specified period.

The **notice** of the forthcoming agm is usually included at the end of the report and accounts, though sometimes it is sent as a separate document. Companies are required to give at least 21 days' notice of the agm so the report and accounts – if it contains the notice of the meeting – must reach shareholders at least three weeks before the agm. In practice, companies normally allow a bit longer for safety.

With the notice of the agm will come a **proxy card**. This has two main purposes. In effect, it allows shareholders who will not be attending the meeting to cast their votes on the resolutions by post. Alternatively, the shareholder may use the proxy card to nominate somebody else to attend the meeting and vote in his place. And the proxy card will say how many shares are cast for or against the different resolutions.

The notice of meeting lists the resolutions to be put to the shareholders at the agm. These resolutions fall into two parts. There are **ordinary resolutions** which deal with routine business. They are likely to include resolutions to:

- receive and consider (or adopt) the **report and accounts**
- **declare a final dividend** on the ordinary shares
- **re-elect directors** who are retiring by rotation or who have joined the board since the last agm
- **reappoint the auditors** or appoint new auditors
- authorise the directors to fix the **auditors' remuneration**.

Agms are not usually contentious affairs and in most cases the resolutions will be passed without opposition. But there are cases where shareholders or a specific group of shareholders are in conflict with the board or perhaps are dissatisfied with the way that the auditors have done their job. They could signify their disapproval by voting not to receive the report and accounts (though this is more a gesture than a vote that necessarily has practical implications). They could, of course, also vote against the reappointment of the auditors. This would have practical implications if they carried the day. They might also vote against the re-election of the directors who are presenting themselves for election. Shareholders also have the right in some circumstances to propose their own resolutions that must be put to the meeting, though the rules are a little complex.

The resolution to declare the **final dividend** is required because, with most companies, the final dividend is merely proposed by the directors and it is not actually paid until shareholders have approved it. If approved, as it almost always is, the cheques will be posted to shareholders shortly after the meeting.

In addition to the ordinary resolutions, the notice of the agm may list certain **special resolutions**. A special resolution is usually required for significant non-routine matters such as changes to the company's **memorandum and articles of association**. We will look at these on page 130.

An **ordinary resolution** succeeds if more than 50% vote in favour. A **special resolution** requires 75% in favour. But these percentages require some explanation. The relevant figures are 50% or 75% of those who vote, not of all those who are entitled to vote and the **voting system** is a little complex. At first the chairman of the meeting will call for a **show of hands** on the resolution, asking for 'all those in favour'. Shareholders who are in favour will stick up an arm. The chairman will then ask for 'those against', at which point dissenters may raise an arm. Most resolutions will be passed unanimously. It is where there is dissent that things can become interesting.

On a show of hands, each shareholder has one vote, whether he owns one share or a million shares. You might have a resolution where 30 people voted in favour and only six against. But the six dissenters might own more shares than the other 30 voters combined. This resolution would be passed on a show of hands. But the dissenters, if they are significant in numbers or size of shareholdings (the rules may be a little complex), may then call for a **poll**.

In a poll it is the votes cast and not just the arms raised that have to be counted. Since most companies have a one-vote-per-ordinary-share capital structure, this normally involves totting up all the shares cast for and against the resolution, including the postal votes received on proxy cards. If this count shows, in the case of an ordinary resolution, that more votes were cast against than for the resolution, the resolution will fail regardless of the fact that it had been approved on a show of hands.

We mentioned earlier the **special resolutions** requiring a 75% vote in favour. These would be required for changes to the company's **constitution**, as set out in its memorandum and articles of association. The notice of meeting should set out the motion, which may be phrased in pretty incomprehensible legalese, but more considerate companies will include an explanation somewhere in the report and accounts. There are, however, some fairly common special resolutions which frequently crop up on the agenda of the agm. These are resolutions granting or renewing powers to the directors to:

- **Issue new shares**. As an additional check on the powers of directors, they need to renew regularly their authority to issue new shares on behalf of the company, however the shares are issued, and whether there is any present intention of issuing new shares or not. The power they seek normally allows them to issue new shares representing not more than a third of existing capital. If they wanted to issue more than this, they would need shareholders' express permission for the issue at the time.
- **Disapply pre-emption rights**. Under the Companies Acts, new shares issued for cash should be offered first to existing shareholders (the **pre-emption principle**). Companies often seek powers to avoid this requirement in respect of small issues of shares which would not (in the directors' view) justify the expense of a full **rights issue**. The number of shares or proportion of the share capital that may be issued in this way will be stated.
- Buy the company's own shares. The Companies Acts effectively prohibit a company from using the company's own money (or providing other **financial assistance**) for the **purchase of its own shares** in most circumstances. However, companies do sometimes think it might be in the interests of shareholders to buy in and cancel shares. They therefore need to seek permission from shareholders to have the power to do this. The resolution is likely to set a low limit on the number of shares that might be acquired in this way and impose fairly stringent conditions for such purchases to avoid abuse.

Incidentally, you will see at the end of the notice of meeting a statement that certain documents are available for inspection up until the date of the agm (probably at the offices of the company's lawyers) and during the meeting itself. These documents will include the **directors' service contracts**, which sometimes make interesting reading for those who can take the trouble.

Part III

What it all means

What to look for in a set of accounts

We've looked at the figures that go to make up a set of accounts. Now it's time to see what these numbers might tell us about a company's progress, its financial stability and its future prospects. Calculating a few of the simple ratios that we've already looked at should help and the movement in the numbers from one year to the next will provide useful clues to what is happening behind the scenes.

If you really want to get to grips with a company's report and accounts, here's a bit of advice. Start with the figures themselves: the **profit and loss account**, **cash flow statement** and **consolidated balance sheet**. The real purist would go even further: read the **notes to the accounts** before you even read the accounts, as that's where any 'nasties' are going to be tucked away, well out of the spotlight. Remember that there are certain things a company must, by law, disclose. But there's no law against companies making generous use of the public relations industry in the way they choose to present material, and most of the bigger ones do. At the same time, check on the **auditor's report** to make sure there are no unpleasant surprises there and have a glance at the note on **accounting policies**. If there have been changes in policies over the year this always deserves a second look.

There's no point in trying to learn accounts interpretation in the abstract. Have a set of accounts in front of you. See first of all what impression you get of the company and its current state of health from the bare figures. It's not easy at first but you develop an instinct for homing in on the important areas once you've looked at a number of different sets of accounts. There will, at the very least, be some points of detail you cannot fully comprehend from the bare figures; but form your own broad impression. Only after that should you begin looking at the **chairman's statement**, **chief executive's review** and **finance director's report** to see if what you find there confirms and amplifies what the figures have told you. They should at least help to explain some of the points of detail that confused you. And, as we've said elsewhere, a really good finance director's report, read in conjunction with the figures, can provide an excellent grounding in the principles of corporate finance in general.

What are you looking for in a set of accounts? It depends who you are of course. Someone who is thinking of doing business with the company is concerned mainly with its financial stability and its ability to pay its bills. But we're looking mainly from the viewpoint of an investor. Would this be a sound company to invest in? The company's financial stability is obviously an important factor. But there is a lot else. And the information in the accounts needs, of course, to be combined with stock market information – the **price of the shares**, their **yield** and **PE ratio** at the very least – to form an investment judgement.

The accounts alone cannot give you the full picture of the company's prospects, let alone whether the shares are good value at their current price. You need to read what the various directors tell you about the trading outlook, the prospects for different areas of the business, planned expansion or acquisitions and so on. But you probably can get from the financial statements themselves a broad idea of whether the company is expanding or contracting, becoming more or less profitable, and whether its finances look robust enough to support whatever it is doing. One final point before you start. Try to establish early on whether the company has made significant **acquisitions** of other businesses – or **disposed of** parts of its own business – during the year. The breakdown in the profit and loss account should give you a clue. Such acquisitions and disposals can complicate comparisons between one year and another and you need always to bear them in mind in interpreting the figures.

Start with the **profit and loss account**, where the **pre-tax profit** figure is a convenient jumping-off point. It's the figure usually quoted first in press reports of a company's results. Are profits up or down? Is any change accounted for mainly by acquisitions or disposals? This may not – in itself – tell you a great deal about the performance of the original business. Were there any one-off **exceptional items** (profits on sale of properties, losses on closure of businesses, perhaps). Look at what the profits would have been if these items are stripped out.

Does a significant proportion of profits come from the group's share in the profits of **associated companies**? If so, bear this in mind. It is unlikely that the whole of this profit has been received in cash, by way of dividend from the associate, so it is in a somewhat different category from profits generated by the group's wholly-owned operations. You can check on the position when you come to look at the cash flow statement.

Then look at **turnover** and see if it has moved in the same direction (and roughly to the same extent) as profits. Or are there signs that times have become tougher, with profits rising by less than turnover? You might calculate the **operating profit margins** at this point and see how they have moved between the two years.

Have a look, too, at the **interest charge** (if any). If it is markedly different from the previous year you'd want to know the reason. If it has risen, is it that interest rates generally have been rising and the company has a lot of floating-rate borrowings? Or is it that the company has increased its borrowings significantly over the year – to finance an acquisition, perhaps, or simply for capital investment? How many times is the interest payment covered by the earnings available to pay it, and has this ratio changed significantly over the year? How far would profits have to fall before they no longer covered the company's interest costs?

Next look at what is perhaps the most important figure of all: the **earnings per share**. And look at the adjusted earnings (where one-off items are stripped out) as well as the 'official' ones. **Adjusted eps** are usually the best measure of how good a job the company is doing for its shareholders. Rising eps hold out the hope of increased **dividends** in the future. The eps figure is not a perfect guide – it can be **massaged** to a certain extent by an unscrupulous management, even without breaching the accounting rules. But whereas managers might get away with this for a year or so, it is far more difficult to tamper with the long-term trend. So at this point it might be a good idea to flip over to the **five-year summary of results** elsewhere in the report and accounts and look at the longer-term trend of earnings as well. You will also want, later, to see whether **cash flow** is following the same trend as earnings – we'll come to that when we look at the cash flow statement.

The amount of profit the company generates for each share is more important than the bare profit figures themselves. Suppose our company had taken over another of similar size and profitability in exchange for shares. This might have had the effect of doubling pre-tax profits once the profits of the newcomer were included. But, because of the new shares issued in the course of the acquisition, these profits have to be spread over a much larger share capital. Depending on how many new shares were issued, the profit earned for each share might actually have dropped even though pre-tax profits had doubled. The short-run effect of the acquisition has thus been to **dilute** the earnings per share.

Then look at the **dividend**. Is it fully covered by earnings? Has it been increased over the year? Has **dividend cover** (earnings per share divided by the dividend per share) risen or fallen? The dividend cover varies a great deal between companies, so it is not possible to quote a 'norm'. A rapidly expanding business might want to retain as much money in the company as possible to finance this expansion so it might pay only small dividends and dividend cover would be high: five times, perhaps. A more mature company with fewer calls on its cash resources might be happy to make larger dividend payments and settle for lower dividend cover: perhaps a figure of twice, or even less. But an investor should always be thinking 'how safe is the dividend; how far would profits have to fall before the payment was no longer covered by earnings?'.

The message given out by the size of the dividend is not always easy to pick up at first glance, and you will want to see later what the directors have to say about the dividend decision, but there are some important points to remember. A dividend payment is not dictated by the level of profits alone. The company must also have the **cash** available to pay its dividend without straining its finances. So have a quick look at the cash position revealed by the balance sheet to reassure yourself on this score. In fact, if a company suffers a temporary setback one year, it may decide not to cut its dividend even if the payment is not covered by available earnings, provided it has adequate cash. This could be an encouraging sign. It might suggest the directors were expecting profits to recover pretty rapidly. On the other hand, remember that company directors are under considerable pressure from investors to deliver a stable and preferably rising flow of income in the form of dividends. Cuts in the dividend are not greeted with joy. If there are signs that the company is putting a strain on its cash resources by maintaining the dividend, you might be a little worried that it is putting its image in the marketplace ahead of its long-term financial health.

After the dividend, look at how much money the company is **ploughing back** into the business. Is it more or less than the previous year? Bear this figure in mind for when you come to look at the company's expansion plans and how they will be financed.

Finally, if the company has **convertible bonds** or **convertible preference shares** in issue, look at what the impact will be on earnings per share on the assumption that these are ultimately converted into share capital (see pages 62–3). The company should give a figure for **fully diluted earnings per share**. Conversion could have the effect of enhancing earnings per share. More often, it will probably dilute them to some extent. This depends on the terms on which the convertible stocks were first issued and how earnings have performed subsequently. The effect may be very small but in some cases it could be quite significant. If there is serious dilution of earnings to come when the stocks are converted, this could imply a brake on the rate of earnings and dividend growth in the future.

Cash flow statement

Have a look next at the **cash flow statement**. This normally gets less attention in the press and from investment analysts than it deserves. It provides a useful bridge from the profit and loss account to the financial position that will be disclosed by the balance sheet and, on occasion, it may sound warning notes and suggest that the company's position is not quite as comfortable as it might have appeared from the profit and loss account alone.

What are you looking for? Well, cash is the lifeblood of business and if it is leaking away the company could be in trouble. So you are looking first to see if the company is generating enough cash internally to sustain its activities and perhaps to finance expansion. There is no reason, of course, why companies should not also raise cash externally – by taking on new loans, perhaps – to finance the purchase of assets or other businesses. Such operations will also be disclosed by the cash flow statement.

The first point to check is whether the company's cash flow from its operations is markedly different from the profits disclosed by the profit and loss account. If it is, you will want to find the reason. Fortunately, this is quite easy. **A note to the accounts** should provide a 'reconciliation' of operating profit to the net cash inflow or outflow. In other words, it starts with the operating profit shown in the profit and loss account, then lists all the items that need to be added or deducted before arriving at the cash flow from operating activities.

The first of these items will probably be **depreciation**. This, remember, is a deduction made from profits before arriving at the operating profit, to allow for the wearing out of plant and equipment over time. But it is an accounting entry. It doesn't involve any movement of cash. So, for the cash flow statement it is added back in. Then there is the question of **stocks**. If the company has had to spend money during the year in increasing the level of stocks that it holds, this will have soaked up cash. So a deduction is made for any increase in stocks. On the other hand, if stock levels had been reduced, this would have released cash and therefore there would be an addition. The position on **debtors** (mainly people owing money to the company for goods supplied but not yet paid for) is rather similar. If debtors have risen, this will have tied up more of the company's cash and a deduction will have to be made for the increase. The position on **creditors** (people to whom the company owes money for goods it has not yet paid for) works the other way round. If the figure for creditors has risen, this means in effect that people are lending more money to the company by way of trade credit. So any increase in creditors has to be added in before arriving at cash flow.

If there have been very large movements in stocks, debtors or creditors you will want to know the reason. It could just be that the scale of the company's business has increased a great deal (look again to see if turnover rose significantly) or it could be that the company has taken over other businesses whose figures are included for the first time. But, depending on the pattern, it could possibly be that the company has allowed its cash management to slip, which is a warning sign (see pages 84–5 for more detail of how companies can get themselves in trouble this way).

After these additions and subtractions, we have the figure for **net cash inflow** (or, just occasionally, outflow) from operating activities, which appears at the top of the cash flow statement. If there is a net cash outflow, it will sound warning bells. How serious the position is will depend on whether it is the result of some one-off exceptional item or reflects an on-going problem.

In addition to the cash inflow from operations there may be some cash coming in from **dividends paid by associated companies**. If this is the case, compare the dividends actually received in cash with the share of the profits of the associates that the company took into its profit and loss account. If the share of associates' profits made up a significant proportion of the group's published profits, but the dividends received from the associates were very small, you might begin to question the 'quality' of the group's profits. This is because a significant proportion of profit is not generating an equivalent amount of cash to finance the group's business.

The next point is to see if the cash inflow covers the 'revenue' expenses of the business that need to be paid in cash. These expenses include the **interest** the company paid and the **tax** it paid at home and overseas. And, though it is shown nowadays further down the cash flow statement, the cash cost of the **dividend** might also be treated as one of the running expenses. Usually the cash inflow will comfortably cover these items. If it does not, you might get a bit worried and start looking for the reasons. You might also question how safe the dividend is in the long run if the company is not generating enough cash to cover it.

Look a bit more closely, too, at the **interest paid** during the year. If it is markedly different from the **interest payable** shown in the profit and loss account, you would again want to know the reason. If the cash flow interest figure is much lower, for example, it might suggest that part of the interest cost incurred by the company during the year was being 'rolled up'. In other words, it was going to be paid later, which might indicate a future drain on cash resources.

See how much of the company's cash inflow is left after deducting the outflows we have mentioned. This remaining figure is the surplus cash the company has generated, after covering its running cash outlays, which is therefore available to help to finance capital investment and for the purchase of additional businesses. Or it may, of course, simply be applied in repaying existing loans or in swelling the cash that the group holds on its balance sheet.

This is what the remainder of the cash flow statement will show you. Under the heading of **capital expenditure and financial investment** you will see what cash the company spent in buying fixed assets during the year and you can work out whether this was covered by the cash generated from operations.

As well as cash outlays you will also see at this point any additional cash the company brought in from the sale of fixed assets. Perhaps it sold a surplus factory building or some outmoded plant.

The next heading is **acquisitions** or **acquisitions and disposals**. Shown here are the cash outflows or inflows resulting from the purchase of additional businesses or the sale of existing ones. Businesses purchased may, of course, have brought some cash with them and this will also be shown here. Note that if a new business was purchased for shares rather than cash, the purchase cost will not show up here because it did not involve cash outlays.

It is always reassuring if a company covers a fair bit of its capital expenditure with cash generated from its own operations. But it may also be perfectly reasonable for a company to run down its existing holdings of cash or to raise fresh loans to finance a heavy capital expenditure programme. And purchases of other businesses are frequently financed with the help of borrowed money. The important point is to look at the effect of capital expenditure and acquisitions on the finances of the company as a whole. If it leads to a marked deterioration in the main financial ratios, which you would look at when you come to the balance sheet, then you might come to the conclusion that the company was over-extending itself financially via its expansion.

At this point a line is drawn and the cash flow statement shows the **net cash inflow** (or **outflow**) **before use of liquid resources and financing**. In other words, the figure shown here is the net result in cash terms of all the company's activities during the year, on both revenue and capital account. If there was an inflow of cash you will want to see how it was used. If there was an outflow you will want to see where the cash came from to cover it.

The next section on **management of liquid resources** is a little technical and may not tell you a great deal that reflects on the company's health. In effect it shows changes in the way the group's cash and near-cash resources are invested. Thus, if cash was used to buy some sort of short-term bond as an investment, this would technically be an outflow of cash into an investment which is not cash. But since the cash is going into something that can readily be turned back into cash, the significance of the change may be limited.

It is when you come to the **financing** heading that you return to the heart of the matter. This shows how the company dealt with the result of everything that has gone before. If the company had a surplus inflow of cash after all its outlays, how did it apply it? And if there was an outflow, where did the necessary cash come from to cover it?

If there was a surplus inflow, it will probably have been used to repay borrowings or may simply have gone to swell the cash in the balance sheet (we will see this right at the end). Borrowings may have had to be repaid, of course, simply because they fell due, even when the company had not generated a cash surplus over the year. If there was a net cash outflow, new loans may have been raised to cover it or new shares may have been issued for cash. Or the company may simply have run down its existing cash resources.

Under the financing heading you will see details of loans repaid or new loans raised and of cash raised from the issue of shares. The net result of all these transactions is shown under the heading of **net inflow** (or **outflow**) **from financing**. This, remember, is different from what you have seen before. It shows the net result of transactions with the outside world; money that has been raised from outside the company or repaid to external lenders.

At the very bottom we come to the heading **Increase** (or **decrease**) **in cash for the period**. This is the bridge that leads to what you will expect to find in the balance sheet. The company might have had a net outflow of cash after covering its revenue and capital spending, but more than covered this via an issue of shares for cash. Provided this was not soaked up by big loan repayments, you would expect to see an increase in cash for the period. Or the company might have raised further large loans, which would have the same effect on cash held but a very different effect on the balance sheet ratios. Or the company might simply have decided to run down its cash holdings, in which case there will have been a decrease in cash for the period.

Balance sheet

Now turn to the **consolidated balance sheet**. If you remember what you have seen in the profit and loss account and the cash flow statement you will know quite a bit of what to expect. If the cash flow statement showed heavy spending on fixed assets, you will expect this figure to have risen significantly. If the company had made a major **acquisition** for cash during the year you will expect all the figures to have risen sharply as the assets and liabilities of the newcomer were incorporated for the first time. If the company had raised or repaid **loans**, you would expect to see this reflected in the figures for **long-term** and **short-term creditors**. If the company had created new shares and sold them to raise cash (perhaps in a rights issue) you would expect to see an increase in **shareholders' funds** as a whole, due to a rise in **issued capital** and in **share premium account**. You would see the same thing (though the implications would be different) if the company had created new shares and used them as currency to buy another business.

Perhaps **shareholders' funds** should be the starting point. Remember that this is the figure that represents the value (for accounting purposes) of the shareholders' interest in the company. When this rises it means that the value of the shareholders' interest has risen, which is usually a good thing (though totally separate from the **market value** of the company, which depends on the share price on the stock exchange). But be careful if shareholders' funds have risen simply or mainly because the company issued shares to buy another business. In this case the total value of the shareholders' interest has risen, but it is now spread over a larger number of shareholders since it includes the new shareholders who sold their own business in exchange for shares. The existing shareholders may not have seen any increase in the value of their proportionate share.

The way to test this, of course, is to calculate the **net asset value per share** or **NAV** (equity shareholders' funds divided by the number of ordinary shares in issue) for the previous year and the latest one. Has it in fact gone up? But before you do this, have a look at the company's **fixed assets**. Do these include any **intangible assets** (probably **goodwill**)? You would normally strip this out by deducting any intangibles from shareholders' funds before arriving at a net tangible asset value per share. Once you have calculated the NAV, see how it compares with the current market price of the shares. Is it high enough to lend support to the share price? And do the company's assets include quantities of readily saleable assets such as properties, that might appeal to a potential takeover bidder?

Then look at the other reasons for whatever movement there is in shareholders' funds. Fortunately, this should be spelled out fairly clearly in the note on movements in shareholders' funds and/or movements in reserves. Here you will see a record of **new shares issued**, of the increase in **issued capital** and in **share premium account** that resulted and of the profit from the year's operations that was ploughed back into the business and therefore accounted for as an addition to the **profit and loss account reserve**. If shareholders' funds rose because of the surplus on a **property revaluation** or something similar, this will be shown here as well. Or perhaps shareholders' funds fell because the group had to sell a subsidiary business at a loss during the year. Or, indeed, because the company made a whacking great trading loss, which resulted in a reduction in the profit and loss account reserve. So you will now know whether the value of existing shareholders' interest in the company rose or not and you will also be able to see why.

The next thing is probably to work out the company's **total borrowings** and also its **net borrowings** (borrowings less cash – see pages 26–7) though you should already have a pretty good idea of what is likely to have happened from what you saw in the cash flow statement. Sometimes cash will exceed borrowings, in which case you have a **net cash position**. If borrowings have risen a great deal, make sure you are clear as to the reason. But to understand the implications of the change you need to do a further calculation to arrive at the gearing, the relationship between borrowed money and shareholders' money in the business. So to arrive at the **net gearing (net borrowings as a percentage of shareholders' funds)** simply multiply the net borrowings figure by 100 and divide it by the equity shareholders' funds (see pages 26–7). Usually you would take the shareholders' funds figure after knocking off goodwill.

What will this gearing figure tell you? Not necessarily a great deal on its own, as the typical **gearing level** varies a lot between different types of business. Even within a particular business sector, different companies have different financing strategies. Some are prepared to use a lot more borrowed money than others. A general rule is that companies with a stable income source, preferably backed by solid assets, can safely run a fairly high level of gearing. Property investment companies are a typical example and gearing of 80% or more might not worry you here. On the other hand, a company in a very volatile business, where profits fluctuate a great deal from year to year, might be less happy with very high gearing. There's far more chance that it might be caught by a severe profits downturn and find itself unable to pay the **interest** on the borrowed money. The position also depends on the level of interest rates at the time and on whether the borrowed money is at a fixed or floating rate of interest. At the time of writing in 2002 interest rates were low by historical standards and quite high borrowings would not necessarily result in interest costs that were a severe strain on profits. But, for the high-geared company with floating-rate borrowings, the position could rapidly look very different if interest rates turned sharply up (see pages 78–9 for some illustrations). And remember that a period of high interest rates is likely to damp down economic activity and company profits, so the interest charges might be moving up as profits moved down, a potentially lethal combination that catches out many companies in a recession. So as well as the gearing shown in the balance sheet, look back at how well interest charges are covered by available profits in the profit and loss account (**income gearing** – see pages 8–9) and work out how far profits would have to fall before the company was unable to pay its interest bill.

Often the most interesting aspect of the gearing is the movement from the previous year. If gearing had shot up from 30% to 60% you'd certainly be worried enough to investigate the reason. Has the company borrowed the cash to buy another business? If so, what are its prospects of getting the gearing back to a more usual level (the **finance director's report**, when you come to it, should help here). Does the increased gearing result from heavy spending on fixed assets? From a movement from profits into losses, with consequent decline in cash flow? From letting stocks or debtors get out of control (see pages 84–5)? The chances of getting gearing under control will depend on the reasons why it rose sharply in the first place.

There are two main ways a company can reduce its gearing in the short run: by selling off parts of its business for cash or by creating and selling new shares for cash. In the first case gearing reduces because the cash can be used to reduce the borrowings side of the gearing equation. In the second case the creation and sale of new shares boosts the shareholders' funds side while the cash raised can also be used to repay borrowings. A big rise in gearing may therefore hint at the likelihood of a **rights issue** – news that is not always good for the share price. It is likely to be particularly damaging if the company is clearly already in dire financial straits and effectively having to ask its shareholders for more money to prevent it from going bust.

Having done these basic calculations, have a look at some of the detail. Remember again that if there has been a major takeover of another company during the year (or a sale of part of the existing business, come to that), this will make it difficult to draw immediate conclusions from big changes in the figures between the previous year and the latest one. You'd expect big changes, because the figures will reflect the new assets brought into the business or the disappearance of the assets of the business that has been sold. So let us assume for convenience that there have been no major acquisitions or sales during the year.

Take **fixed assets** first. Have tangible fixed assets risen significantly, suggesting heavy **capital expenditure** (which might be good for future profits)? Have **tangible assets** increased simply because the company has revalued its properties upwards (it is always good to know they are worth more than you earlier thought, but it does not actually tell you anything much about the company's investment policy)? Have there been any significant sales of assets? You'll find quite a lot of detail in the note to the accounts on fixed assets, which ought to give you the picture.

Are there also **intangible assets** included among fixed assets and, if so, do they represent a significant proportion of the fixed assets total? The most common form of intangible asset is, of course, **goodwill** acquired in the course of the takeover of another company, when the price paid is higher than the **net assets** that the newcomer brings with it (see pages 88–9). So, if there have been no takeovers during the year, the figure for goodwill is unlikely to have risen. But acquired goodwill is not the only possible type of intangible asset. Things like patents, trade marks or licences that the company owns may also have a value put on them and be shown as an intangible asset. So might, say, the title of a national newspaper that belongs to a publishing company.

There are really two main points to consider on intangibles. If there is a big goodwill item, remember that it will normally be knocked off before calculating **net tangible assets**. And it may also need to be **depreciated**, which will be a charge against profits. Opinions vary on how other types of intangible should be treated; whether they should be knocked off before calculating net assets. A patent might be readily saleable and, in fact, have a clear market value. So it might be treated more like a tangible asset.

The second point is whether the intangibles are really worth the figures at which they are shown in the balance sheet. For example, if a mobile phone company spends megabucks in acquiring new-generation mobile phone licences, the licences would be an intangible asset. But if the bottom drops out of the mobile phone market, these licences might in practice turn out to be worth a lot less than was paid for them. Companies are meant to write down the value of their intangible assets if there has been a serious and permanent fall (**impairment**) in value. Whether they always do so is a moot point.

Next, have a look at investments, if there are any. These could take a lot of different forms. Perhaps the two types you should look at most closely are investments in **associated companies** and investments in the company's **own shares**. Has the group taken significant stakes in other businesses during the year? Has it increased its investment in existing associated companies? Remember that the value you see under 'associated companies' is the group's share of the net assets of these companies. The group may also have made loans to these companies (or guaranteed loans taken out by these companies) so its total investment, or the total amount for which it is at risk, could be a lot higher. The details of **creditors** would show whether there are loans to the associated companies and the note on **contingent liabilities** should show any guarantees provided for loans.

Investment in own shares almost certainly represents shares in the company held by an employee share ownership plan or **ESOP** (see page 119). If the figure is large it might sound a warning note. If our company hits problems, the value of its shares will fall. This then knocks the value of the shares that it owns in itself, which reduces net assets and might help the share price to fall further, and so on. It has happened!

Next, we have the **working capital** position: the short-term assets and liabilities of the business and the relationship between them. Since 'working capital' seems to mean slightly different things to different people, we won't try to define it too rigidly. It is basically the money needed to finance the company's day-to-day operations rather than its long-term assets. And management of working capital is a crucial part of any company's business – there's an example of how things can go wrong on pages

84–5. So the company has laid out money to buy stocks of materials and finance the production of finished goods. It has provided goods to customers, some of whom have not yet paid (**trade debtors**), and in the meantime it has had to bear the cost of producing these goods. This ties up money, too. Against this, in effect it has temporary loans from people who have supplied it with goods or services and have not yet been paid (trade creditors). So one of the sums you can do is to take the total of stocks plus short-term debtors and deduct the figure for creditors. This is one measure of the money tied up as working capital of the business and you can see how it has moved between the previous year and the latest one. If the company's business has been expanding, as reflected in its turnover, the chances are that the figure has risen. If it has changed radically for other reasons, you will want to see what these are.

Look first at the figure for **net current assets** (or, more rarely, **net current liabilities**) as a whole. These are the current assets less the current liabilities and again any radical movements will need explanation if they are not simply a reflection of the expansion of the business. It is not necessarily a sign of impending doom if a company's short-term creditors exceed its short-term assets to result in net current liabilities. You could have a company whose business requires very little in the way of stocks (on the asset side) but which derives much of its finance from short-term loans (on the liabilities side). But a swing from a position of net current assets to net current liabilities, or any marked deterioration in the ratio, would certainly merit investigation. Is it because cash holdings have been run down? Is it because short-term borrowings have risen sharply or moved from the long-term to the short-term debt category because they are now repayable within a year? Either of these changes could sound a warning note. Is it that **trade creditors** have risen much more sharply than **trade debtors**? The message here is not necessarily so clear cut. It could be that the company is managing its cash rather cleverly, effectively saving cash by persuading its suppliers to wait longer for payment while avoiding any offsetting increase in the time it waits for payment from its customers. On the other hand, it could be that creditors have increased sharply because the company is having trouble in paying its bills, and this would be a definite sign of trouble. You should be able to judge from your general picture of the state of the company and from what you read elsewhere in the report and accounts. If cash holdings have been run right down you would incline to the more pessimistic assumption.

Under the current assets heading an increase in **debtors** that is vastly disproportionate to the growth of business is rarely an encouraging sign. It could mean that the company is having increasing problems in getting its customers to pay on time which could reflect a deterioration in its market clout and bargaining position. Or it could be that the company has simply become lax in chasing up the money owing to it. Either way, it is soaking up that vital cash.

Movements in **stocks** also need a close look if they are out of line with the growth (or shrinkage) in the company's operations. If they have risen inexplicably, look at the detail in the notes to see if the increase has been mainly in raw materials, work in progress or finished goods. A big increase in raw materials held might suggest that the company has been lax and tied up more of its cash in stocks than is strictly necessary for efficient operation. A big increase in finished goods held would definitely be worrying if it is not adequately explained. Is the company manufacturing products that it is having trouble in selling?

Whether it is debtors or stocks that have risen disproportionately (or both!), look at the third main component of current assets, cash. All else being equal the figure for cash is likely to have fallen as it has been soaked up in the financing of increased debtors or stocks. This would not, in itself, affect the total figure for current assets. But it would be a worrying migration from one category of short-term asset to another.

From short-term assets and liabilities, move on to the longer-term liabilities of the business, shown under **creditors (amounts falling due after more than one year).** You will have noticed in your first over-view of the balance sheet whether these have risen or fallen over the past year. Now you will need to look at the notes to the accounts to find out a bit more of the detail. There's more information on the categorisation of debt on page 97. Here, the questions you are trying to answer are: how soundly is the company financed and what are the implications of its debt financing structure for the future?

First point: what is the **maturity of the debt** (i.e. when do the borrowings have to be repaid)? If a major part of the debt is due for repayment in eighteen months, it will move over to the short-term debt category next year. How will existing borrowings be replaced when they fall due? If the company has been going through a bad trading patch it might not find it too easy to raise fresh loans on acceptable terms. And an allied point: does the company have any arrangements in place for raising further money when needed? There might be information on additional borrowing facilities that are already in place in the note or in the finance director's report.

Second, is most of the debt at **fixed** or **floating rates of interest** and what sort of **interest rates** is the company paying? A lot of debt at floating rates of interest brings the risk of big increases in interest costs – which could bash profits severely – if interest rates generally move up significantly in the future. Of course, there could equally be a boost to profits if interest rates move down. Borrowings at fixed rates of interest are in one sense safer: the company knows what it will be paying over the coming years. If it raised the fixed-interest money when rates were higher than today's it equally means that it will be paying over the odds for some time to come. But be a bit careful in drawing hasty conclusions. There are various types of 'insurance' or financial instrument a company can use to limit the maximum interest it could have to pay on floating-rate debt or to swap floating-rate into fixed-rate, or vice versa. You should find details of **hedges** that the company has used against the interest rate risk either in the note or in the finance director's report.

Third, in what currencies has the company borrowed? If most of its operations are in the UK but it has borrowed heavily in US dollars, the loans are going to cost more to repay in terms of sterling if the value of the dollar rises against the pound. But again, look at whether the company has taken out any form of insurance against the currency risk.

Finally, if the company has any **convertible loans**, look at the conversion terms and what the impact on the balance sheet will be if the loans are converted. Comparing the conversion price with the company's current share price will help to give some idea of the likelihood of conversion. If the share price is already above the conversion price it is likely that the convertible loan will be turned into shares at some point which will have the effect of reducing the company's gearing by replacing debt with equity. But it might also have the effect of diluting the company's net asset value (see pages 60–3 for an explanation and the calculations).

By this time you should have a pretty good feel for the soundness (or otherwise!) of the company's finances and whether they are adequate for whatever plans it has in mind. But before you leave the balance sheet, just have a further quick glance through the notes to the accounts to see if there are any unpleasant surprises. Does the company have a big shortfall on its **pension fund**, for example, or are there any possible large future liabilities lurking under **contingent liabilities**? Once you've satisfied yourself on these points, you may check your own impressions against the explanations given by the finance director in the **financial review** and against the other narrative parts of the report and accounts.

Reading the Austin Reed accounts

Having looked at the principles of reading a set of accounts, we are going to apply them now to a real company. The company is clothing retailer Austin Reed and its financial year runs to 31 January. The accounts we are looking at are for the year to 31 January 2001. We will refer to this year as 2000–01.

A little history helps to set the scene. Austin Reed, with its flagship store in London's Regent Street, used to be both a retailer and manufacturer of up-market clothing. Its manufacturing operations had, in common with others, been going through a rough patch in recent years. It decided to dispose of them and shed its last manufacturing operation, at a loss, in its 2000–01 financial year. This has cast something of a pall over the 2000–01 figures. But we may find that the position is rather better than it looks at first glance.

The company now describes itself, formally, in the directors' report as a 'specialist retailer and licensor of quality business and leisure clothing for men and women'. But within this business it has also had to adapt to changing social trends. The move is away from formal clothing, which was one of Austin Reed's strengths, towards a more casual style. It has been changing its product mix accordingly and concentrating on developing new ranges of smart 'casual' clothing. It operates under the 'Austin Reed' and 'Country Casuals' brand names and has stores, or concessions in other company's stores, throughout the United Kingdom. It also derives an income from licensing its products overseas.

First, what does the profit and loss account tell us?

Turnover is up very slightly from £113.6m to £114.6m (see page 144), but of this figure some £4.8m relates to the manufacturing businesses prior to their sale. Their turnover will not appear in future years. The turnover from continuing operations was therefore £109.7m. We can read in the financial review that sales from continuing retail businesses actually increased by 5% over the year.

Operating expenses were also up over the year, but the group was still able to increase its **operating profits** slightly from £7.85m to £7.9m. The 'discontinued operations' – the manufacturing businesses – made an operating loss of £369,000 during the part of the year that they still belonged to the group. This loss will not recur. If it is 'stripped out' of the figures, the operating profit from continuing operations is higher at £8.34m. This is the significant figure because it tells us most about the profit-earning capability of the group in its present form.

Against the operating profit there is a very hefty **one-off** item to set. This is the loss of £6.33m on the disposal of the manufacturing operations. The notes to the accounts show that the group received £3.71m from the sale (with the possibility of a little more to come), but this was far exceeded by the £10m that had been invested in one way and another in the manufacturing businesses. Remember that the **official earnings figures** have to take account of this loss.

After paying **interest** of £1.57m (not greatly different from the previous year) Austin Reed shows a **profit before tax** of £6.77m before the exceptional loss but only £72,000 after it. The note on **segmental analysis** reveals that profits from retail operations were £7.41m and from licensing £1.91m, against which there were common costs of £2.55m to be set, leaving the figure of £6.77m.

Profits after tax come out at £5.03m before the exceptional loss and only £57,000 after it. But be careful if you are going to calculate your own **earnings per share** figures. You cannot tell it from the face

Consolidated profit and loss account
For the year ended 31 January 2001

	Note	2001 Continuing operations £'000	2001 Discontinued operations £'000	2001 Total £'000	2000 Continuing operations £'000	2000 Discontinued operations £'000	2000 Total £'000
Turnover	2	109,710	4,847	114,557	104,365	9,232	113,597
Cost of sales		(50,565)	(4,177)	(54,742)	(49,209)	(6,839)	(56,048)
Gross profit		59,145	670	59,815	55,156	2,393	57,549
Operating expenses and other income	3 & 26	(50,810)	(1,039)	(51,849)	(47,815)	(1,651)	(49,466)
Exceptional operating expenses and other income		–	–	–	(233)	–	(233)
Operating profit		8,335	(369)	7,966	7,108	742	7,850
Profit on disposal of fixed assets		–	–	–	344	–	344
Loss on disposal of business	7	–	(6,325)	(6,325)	–	–	–
Loss on termination of operations		–	–	–	–	(4,661)	(4,661)
		8,335	(6,694)	1,641	7,452	(3,919)	3,533
Interest payable	4	(1,569)	–	(1,569)	(1,571)	–	(1,571)
Profit on ordinary activities before taxation	2 & 5	6,766	(6,694)	72	5,881	(3,919)	1,962
Taxation	7 & 8	(1,735)	1,720	(15)	(2,037)	1,421	(616)
Profit on ordinary activities after taxation		5,031	(4,974)	57	3,844	(2,498)	1,346
Dividends paid and proposed	9	(2,438)	–	(2,438)	(2,345)	–	(2,345)
Retained profit/(loss) for the financial year	22	2,593	(4,974)	(2,381)	1,499	(2,498)	(999)
Basic and fully diluted earnings per share							
Adjusted to exclude exceptional items	10	16.0p		15.2p	12.2p		14.2p
Including exceptional items	10	16.0p		0.1p	12.2p		4.2p

During the year the Group disposed of the remaining part of its manufacturing division to Thompson Holdings (London) Limited. The trading results for the division are shown separately above together with the exceptional costs of disposal.

of the profit and loss account, but the note on dividends shows that Austin Reed has **preference shares** as well as **ordinary shares** in issue. The cost of the **preference dividend** is quite small – a mere £27,000 – but it still has to be knocked off the net profit after tax (**Profit on ordinary activities after taxation**) before arriving at the profit attributable to ordinary shareholders (**equity earnings**) on which the **earnings per share** or **eps** calculation is made.

Austin Reed paid an **interim dividend** of 2.5p per ordinary share during the year and proposes a **final dividend** of 5.25p for shareholders' approval. The total payment for the year is therefore 7.75p (a small advance on the previous year's 7.5p) and the cost of dividends, including the small preference dividend we have mentioned, is £2.44m. The ordinary dividend, we can calculate, is **covered** 2.08 times by earnings from continuing operations and before the exceptional loss on the sale of the manufacturing business, which is healthy enough. But it is clearly not covered by profits after the exceptional items so it is being paid mainly from **reserves** and this will show up as a reduction in **shareholders' funds** in the balance sheet.

Earnings per share are shown by the company as being 16p if the exceptional loss is excluded and only continuing operations are taken into account. Allowing for the operating loss from the manufacturing operations (which will not recur) the figure comes down to 15.2p and right back to an **official earnings** figure of 0.1p after knocking off the losses on the sale of the manufacturing businesses. It is the 16p that probably gives the best indication of the normal earnings capability of the company in its present shape.

Cash flow

The first thing to note about Austin Reed's **cash flow statement** is that it presents a very healthy picture, which is only partly due to the sale of the manufacturing businesses. **Net cash inflow** of £10.7m from operating activities is well in excess of operating profit. The notes to the accounts underline one of the main reasons, which is also referred to in the financial review. Careful control of inventory levels has enabled the company to reduce the level of **stocks** that it held at the year-end by some £2.81m. This has therefore released **cash** which had earlier been tied up in higher levels of stock.

Interest paid and **preference dividends** together soak up £1.59m of the cash generated from operations. The interest actually paid during the year was different from the interest payable that was shown in the profit and loss account, but only marginally so. The **tax** of £1.18m actually paid during the year was also different from the tax payable shown in the profit and loss account, and in this case the difference is quite large but probably not of great significance.

We can calculate that interest, preference dividends and tax together absorbed £2.77m of the net cash inflow and if we add in the £2.33m cash used to pay equity dividends (actually shown lower down the statement) the total comes to £5.1m. This still leaves £5.6m of the original cash inflow of £10.7m available for other purposes. The equity dividends in question are the past year's interim and the previous year's final, which were the payments actually made during the financial year. The past year's final had yet to be approved by shareholders before it would be paid. Note that, while the **dividend** was not covered by profits after exceptional losses on the sale of the manufacturing businesses (as we saw in the profit and loss account) it is more than adequately covered by the cash that the company is generating. This makes it look considerably safer.

Next we turn from the revenue to the capital items. Austin Reed spent £3.33m on buying **fixed assets** during the year, partially offset by £400,000 received from the sale of fixed assets. This **capital expenditure** is therefore comfortably covered out of the year's remaining £5.6m cash inflow. But in addition we see under the heading of **acquisitions and disposals** that the sale of the manufacturing businesses brought in cash of £3.71m, offset by sales costs of £595,000 for a net cash receipt of £3.12m.

Cash flow statement
For the year ended 31 January 2001

	Note	2001 £'000	2000 £'000
Net cash inflow from operating activities	24	10,695	7,426
Returns on investments and servicing of finance			
Interest paid		(1,561)	(1,834)
Preference dividends paid		(27)	(23)
		(1,588)	(1,857)
Taxation		(1,176)	(1,789)
Capital expenditure and financial investment			
Purchase of tangible fixed assets		(3,332)	(1,831)
Sale of tangible fixed assets		400	1,467
Purchase of own shares for LTIP trust		–	(190)
		(2,932)	(554)
Acquisition and disposals			
Sale of business		3,712	–
Disposal costs		(595)	–
		3,117	–
Equity dividends paid		(2,333)	(2,322)
Net cash inflow before financing		5,783	904
Financing			
Reduction in debt		–	(2,907)
		–	(2,907)
Increase/(reduction) in cash in the year		5,783	(2,003)

Reconciliation of net cash flow to movement in net debt		£'000	£'000
Increase/(reduction) in cash in the year		5,783	(2,003)
Cash outflow from movement in net debt		–	2,907
Movement in net funds in the year		5,783	904
Net debt at beginning of year		(17,908)	(18,812)
Net debt at end of year	25	(12,125)	(17,908)

The net effect of all these inflows and outflows is that Austin Reed had a **net inflow** of £5.78m of cash before **financing transactions**. It had no need to raise fresh cash from external sources and, indeed, the 'surplus' cash flow allowed it to reduce its **net debt** from £17.91m to £12.13m over the year, as you can see at the bottom of the statement. We'll see the effects of this debt reduction when we come to look at the balance sheet. In the meantime, remember that – all else being equal – interest charges should be lower in the subsequent year as a result of the lower net borrowings.

Balance sheet

Now to the **balance sheet**. The first point to note is that the figures reflect the disappearance from the accounts of the assets and liabilities of the manufacturing businesses that have been disposed of. This results in a reduction from £41.6m to £39m in **tangible fixed assets**, despite the £3.33m spent on buying fixed assets that we noted in the cash flow statement. The notes tell us that some £26m of the fixed assets is represented by the group's **freehold and long leasehold properties**, which would be readily marketable assets – not that Austin Reed shows any signs of wanting to get rid of them!

The figures for **current assets** and **current liabilities** are also down overall, though their composition has changed. The most notable difference is the rise from £412,000 to £6.98m in the amount of **cash** Austin Reed holds under current assets. This arises partly from the cash released by reducing the level of stocks held, which we noted earlier. The sale of the manufacturing businesses will also have removed the stocks that they held so that, overall, the stocks level has reduced very significantly.

When we come to **creditors (amounts falling due within one year)** we have to look at the notes for the detail. The rather surprising thing, given the strong cash flow, is that **short-term borrowings** shown here have actually risen from £877,000 to £3.62m. They comprise a **bank overdraft** and a **term loan**. However, there is a simple reason for the size of the increase. We'll see when we come to long-term creditors that Austin Reed has a term loan, repayable by instalments, that are now beginning. An instalment of £1.96m has now become due within the next year, so this amount has simply moved from long-term liabilities to short-term ones.

Indeed, this term loan is the only item under **creditors (amounts falling due after one year)** and it has reduced from £17.44m to £15.48m as the instalment due within a year has moved to short-term liabilities. The term loan was originally for seven years, and we can see from the repayment schedule provided that a further £3.66m is repayable between one and two years off and the remaining £11.82m is repayable between two and five years off. Will this repayment schedule pose any problems? Well, Austin Reed has plenty of cash at the moment and it is currently generating cash at a good rate as well. So the position looks fairly comfortable unless it goes in for a massive capital expenditure programme.

There is further useful information on **borrowings** in the notes. The term loan is in sterling though the group has just over £1m of its short-term borrowings in US dollars. And all its borrowings are at **floating rates of interest**. On the face of it, Austin Reed might be vulnerable to an upturn in interest rates. But then we see that it had 'taken out insurance' against this risk by buying an **interest rate cap** which puts a top limit on the rate of interest it might have to pay. But this cap arrangement was due to run out a month after the company's financial year-end, so we do not know if it was renewed or not. The financial review simply says that interest rate risks are **hedged** where 'appropriate'. All borrowings are **secured** by a **fixed charge** on Austin Reed's properties, incidentally.

Since we are looking at debt, perhaps we might at this point work out Austin Reed's **gearing** (the relationship between shareholders' money and borrowed money in the business – see pages 26–7). Long- and short-term borrowings together amount to £19.1m against £18.3m the previous year. These are the **gross borrowings**. If we then deduct the cash the group holds, we get **net debt** of £12.13m for the latest year against £17.91m a year earlier – a considerable improvement in the group's financial position.

Balance sheets
As at 31 January 2001

	Note	2001 Group £'000	2000 Group £'000	2001 Company £'000	2000 Company £'000
Fixed assets					
Tangible assets	11	39,032	41,564	–	–
Investments	12	136	125	35,006	43,943
		39,168	41,689	35,006	43,943
Current assets					
Stocks	13	16,233	24,567	–	–
Debtors	14	17,851	19,669	22,971	22,527
Bank		6,981	412	6,834	–
		41,065	44,648	29,805	22,527
Creditors					
Amounts falling due within one year	15	19,244	20,182	5,871	3,091
		19,244	20,182	5,871	3,091
Net current assets		21,821	24,466	23,934	19,436
Total assets less current liabilities		60,989	66,155	58,940	63,379
Creditors					
Amounts falling due after one year	16	15,483	17,443	15,483	17,443
Provision for liabilities and charges	18	1,269	2,280	–	37
		16,752	19,723	15,483	17,480
Net assets		44,237	46,432	43,457	45,899
Capital and reserves					
Called up share capital	19	8,194	8,194	8,194	8,194
Share premium	20	2,661	2,661	2,661	2,661
Revaluation reserve	21	18,169	18,147	27,746	32,882
Retained profit	22	15,213	17,430	4,856	2,162
Total shareholders' funds	23	44,237	46,432	43,457	45,899
Equity shareholders' funds		43,891	46,086	43,111	45,553
Non-equity shareholders' funds		346	346	346	346
Total shareholders' funds		44,237	46,432	43,457	45,899

Next look at **shareholders' funds**. The group has a small amount – £346,000 – of **preference capital (non-equity shareholders' funds)**, but this is shareholders' money, though not equity shareholders' money. The total shareholders' money in the business is £44.24m and **gross borrowings as a percentage** of this are 44.2%. More important, however, **net borrowings** are equal to only 27.4% of shareholders' funds. The corresponding figures for the previous year were gross gearing of 39% and net gearing of 36%. On the crucial net gearing measure there has been a very substantial reduction.

Now to the detail of the shareholders' funds. There have been no changes to **issued capital (called-up share capital)** or to **share premium account**. The group has made no share issues over the year. There has also been no significant overall movement in **revaluation reserve** (we can see from the note on tangible assets that the group's properties were revalued on 31 January 1999 and have not been revalued again since). They might now be worth somewhat more than the book figures. The only significant change in shareholders' funds is the reduction from £17.43m to £15.21m in **profit and loss account reserves**, which has led to the reduction in the total figure for shareholders' money. This, remember, was caused by the fact that Austin Reed had net profits of only £57,000 after deducting the exceptional loss during the year, so most of the £2.44m it paid as dividends had to come out of reserves, not out of the year's profit, and reserves are reduced accordingly.

A couple of final points. We can calculate a **net asset value per share**. There is no **goodwill** to knock off, so it is simply a matter of deducting the **preference share capital** from the total of shareholders' funds and dividing the remaining £43.89 of equity shareholders' funds by the number of ordinary shares in issue which, we can see from the notes, is 31.39m shares of 25p par value. The result is an **NAV** of 139.8p per share. This is interesting, as it is significantly higher than the average price of the shares in the market over the group's 2000-01 financial year. In other words, the shares had been trading at a **discount to assets**. And a last check. Look at the notes to see if there's anything nasty lurking under the heading of **contingent liabilities** (see page 96). No, there isn't. No massive lawsuits against the company, or anything on those lines. We can rest easy on that score!

The conclusion

So what can we deduce from the Austin Reed accounts? The best way to approach this is to play 'devil's advocate' and look for any worrying features first. It was a pity that the last of the manufacturing operations had to be sold at a loss. And it's a pity that the dividend was not covered by profits after exceptional losses. But these are in the past. They are the sort of events that are unlikely to recur. If we ignore them, the accounts present a healthy picture. The dividend was well covered by profits before the exceptional items and the dividend increase is perhaps an encouraging sign. Cash flow is healthy and the balance sheet shows a strong cash position as well as a useful reduction in net gearing.

The group's borrowings are mainly in the form of the term loan and the last of this does not have to be repaid for a few years. There are instalment repayments to be met in the meantime, but these seem unlikely to pose major problems. If the group wants to raise fresh loans to replace borrowings that have to be repaid, it seems unlikely to encounter problems. The level of gearing is not high enough to worry a lender and the properties provide security for borrowings. Austin Reed has shown itself cautious in limiting its interest-rate risk by using a cap. And the reduction it has managed to achieve in its stock levels shows that it is aware of the need for tight cash management. Finally, that high net asset value, backed by properties in the balance sheet, lends support to the share price and would certainly have appeal for a potential bidder. As it happens, Austin Reed had talked to a number of companies about the possibility of their taking it over, but decided that it would do better by building up its retail brand and remaining independent.

So the accounts appear to provide a strong base for Austin Reed's operations and suggest it has the finance it needs to continue its programme of developing clothing brands and revamping its stores. How successful it will be in changing its product mix to meet changes in public tastes will emerge only with time and the accounts cannot give the answer here. But they suggest that there is nothing in the company's financial structure to hold the management back. And as it happens – though we wouldn't have known this at the time – Austin Reed's profits for the first half of its 2001–02 financial year did show a significant advance.

Part IV

Removing the veil

How they fiddle the figures

It would be good to feel that all companies and all their directors are honest. Alas, they are not. And even the honest ones may be forgiven for putting a favourable interpretation on their company's situation in preference to an unfavourable one. Figures can be, and are, **massaged** to give the best impression. Where this goes too far we tend to talk of **window-dressing**. Where it goes beyond window-dressing to actually falsifying the figures, there are other terms for it. **Fraud** springs to mind.

The shareholder's main line of defence against directors who go too far in massaging the figures or who actually falsify them is the **auditors**, whose job it is (in Britain) to say whether or not they think that these figures give a **true and fair view**. Companies are required to conform to accounting standards or justify any departure from them in arriving at the figures, but the auditors should also be looking at the principles involved to form a view of whether the end result accurately portrays the company's situation. In America the auditing system works a little differently and is geared more to checking that companies have conformed to a set of precise accounting rules. But, as the scandal of American energy group **Enron** showed when it erupted in 2001, neither auditors nor the accounting rules are always a perfect defence.

The accounting rules in Britain have been tightened up a great deal by the **Accounting Standards Board** in the last decade of the 20th century and since. This followed some very prominent company débâcles in the 1980s, which rarely showed auditors in a good light. Whether an Enron-type scandal could erupt in Britain remains to be seen. It's probably more difficult for accounts to present a misleading impression of the facts than it would have been in the past. But shareholders need to rely on their own wits and observation as well as on the auditors.

Which are the main areas where accounts sometimes set out to deceive, or at least to flatter? There are a couple of points to get clear at the outset. What we refer to as **profit** is a pretty elastic concept. To arrive at the profit for the year, a number of assumptions have to be made: about whether customers are going to pay up or not, for a start, and about the value of stocks at the year-end. Cash flow is different from profit, because it is a fact, and therefore can be more objectively recorded. Suppose you are undertaking a two-year construction project. When are you earning your profit on the contract? Have you earned any profit when you have done half the work? Or can you not take in any profit until the project is complete, the client has paid and you know exactly what your own costs were? This is an extreme example, and the accounting rules provide an answer up to a point. But similar questions crop up with a lot of commercial transactions. So there is an inevitable element of opinion and assumption.

Less scrupulous companies can use this to their advantage. The profit on transactions may be taken early to flatter the current year's figures, or it may be postponed because you know you are going to have problems in producing good figures for the next year. The financial institutions such as life assurance companies and pension funds are the biggest shareholders in UK listed companies. They like the companies they invest in to produce a steady upward trend in earnings and dividends. They don't like too many fluctuations up and down. Companies tend to oblige by **smoothing** their profit figures. If it looks like being a bad year they will tend to bring profit forward to even out. If it looks like being a good year they may tend to defer taking some of the profit so that they have it in reserve for more difficult times later. Within bounds, this smoothing is accepted. It's when the same principle is carried to extremes that the trouble occurs.

Suppose Payola Perfumes plc wants to get its share price up. It brings forward every possible item of profit that it can into the current year's figures, which therefore look excellent and earn plaudits from the financial press. The shares shoot up. But this does not help Payola Perfumes unless it makes use of its artificially high share price. This is because a company can massage its earnings figures in the short run but it is far more difficult to do it over a long timespan. So Payola Perfumes knows perfectly well that it may be able to flatter its profit figures for a year or so with accounting trickery. But in the long run the truth will out. It will hit a year where there is no more profit to be taken. So what Payola Perfumes will probably do is to use its inflated shares as currency to make a takeover bid for another company in the same line of business, which it will therefore be acquiring on the cheap. With the two companies combined it will be far more difficult to make comparisons between two years' performance, and with any luck Payola's earlier accounting trickery will be safely buried.

Be particularly wary if you are ever presented with a set of **pro-forma** figures in a company document. These show what the company's position would be (or might be!) if a particular set of circumstances came to pass. They are sometimes used quite legitimately in, say, a takeover document to show what the effect on the accounts would be if the figures for the two companies were put together, as if the takeover had already occurred. Since these pro-forma accounts are likely to be based on the most recent published accounts for the two companies, they can be helpful.

But be a lot more cynical if you come across a set of pro-forma figures described as something like 'Illustration of possible future profits trend'. The figures are prepared, possibly for five years ahead, based on certain assumptions. 'If turnover increases at 50 per cent a year and if the ratio of costs to sales remains roughly the same, then this is how profits *might* work out over the next five years...' (our italics!). The picture presented is almost invariably rosy. But note a few important points. These are not audited figures. The assumptions will usually be the directors' own. And the directors will be very careful not to present this pro-forma projection of profits as a **forecast**, because the stock exchange has strict rules on the making of forecasts. You are most likely to come across this sort of thing in the prospectus of a very young company launching on the stock exchange before it has an established profits record to work on. But, as may often be the intention, would-be investors tend to view these figures in the light of a forecast all the same. They are often complete bunkum and the outcome rarely matches the projections.

The second main area where accounts may set out to deceive relates to the **balance sheet**. Remember always that the balance sheet shows the company's position on only one day – the last day – of its financial year. The position could look very different on any one of the other 364 days. So, again, a fair bit of **window-dressing** may go on. Back in the 1970s London was host to a number of financial institutions euphemistically referred to as 'secondary banks'. They lent money, particularly for property transactions, but were not recognised banks. Most of them collapsed in the property and financial crisis of the middle years of that decade. It appeared afterwards that a number of them had been able to present an illusory picture of financial strength because certain large deposits were being shuffled between them. The first 'bank' would have the deposits on the day its accounts were drawn up. Once the auditors were out of the way, the same deposits could be on-lent to another 'bank' whose year-end was a few months later. This 'bank' would on-lend it to a third 'bank' once its own audit was out of the way. And so on. So the same pot of money was lending respectability to the balance sheets of a number of different banks and creating a false impression of strength!

This is an extreme example, but more modest window-dressing goes on at many companies. A company whose trade is seasonal, for example, may choose as its financial year-end the time of year when its stocks are at their lowest. Its cash position may look quite strong as a result. What the balance sheet does not tell you is that, for much of the rest of the year, its cash is tied up in far higher levels of stocks and its cash position would look much tighter. Other companies may simply make sure they run their stock levels down as low as possible at the balance sheet date.

There are a number of more specific tricks that companies may use to flatter their figures. Take **depreciation** first. An hotel company, say, might normally have depreciated the furniture and fittings in its hotels over an estimated life of three years. So if it had furniture and fittings of £100m in the balance sheet, it would have to set against its profits a depreciation charge of £33.3m each year. But times are hard and profits are hard to come by. So it suddenly 'discovers' that its furniture and fittings have a longer life than it had thought and should be depreciated over five years instead. This brings the annual depreciation charge down to £20m and profits are boosted by £13.3m as a result. At least one major hotel group did this when it was under severe financial pressure in the 1970s. Companies are nowadays required to draw attention to any change in accounting policies over the year, so you should be able to spot if this kind of thing is going on. It's one reason why you should always have a look at the **accounting policies page** that normally appears close to the main financial statements.

Depreciation may be manipulated in other ways. Where a company has acquired goodwill (see pages 88–9) on its balance sheet it is meant to depreciate or **amortise** it unless it can establish that this goodwill is actually holding or increasing its value. This involves a judgement as to whether the businesses in question are becoming more valuable or less so. There's room for a fair bit of opinion here, leading to the suspicion that some companies may be failing to depreciate goodwill when they should be doing so, and thereby flattering their profits. It is partly because of the different attitude towards depreciation of goodwill at different companies that many investment analysts like to use the **EBITDA** definition of profits when comparing one company with another. This stands for **earnings before interest, taxation, depreciation and amortisation** and thus produces a measure of earnings that is not distorted by different depreciation policies at different companies.

Goodwill is not, of course, the only form of **intangible** asset. Other items that crop up fairly frequently are **patents, trade marks, licences, publication titles** and the like. Always have a look at these and ask yourself if they are likely to have been holding their value. The new-generation mobile phone licences, for which telecoms companies paid such vast sums, began to look considerably less valuable not so long after as evidence emerged of a sharp slowdown in the rate of growth in the mobile phones market. Have the companies concerned recognised this by writing down the value of the licences that they hold?

One other item that always repays a look is any **capitalised expenditure** that is carried on the balance sheet. This appears to have been the central issue in the accounting fiddles that emerged in 2002 at US communications giant **WorldCom**. The general rule in Britain is that all expenses that are incurred in a year must be charged against profits in that year. But an exception is allowed for the costs of developing a particular identifiable project where the revenue that will come from that project in the future is reasonably assured. If this sounds complicated, take an example. A publishing company spends £5m in developing a new magazine for which it has a large number of subscribers lined up in advance. Instead of charging this £5m against profits in the year in which the money is spent, which will reduce profits at a time when no revenue is yet coming in from the magazine, the company **capitalises** this £5m. In other words it does not charge the expenditure against its profits (which has the effect of improving profits by £5m) but treats it as part of the capital cost of the project. It will appear as an intangible asset in the balance sheet under a heading something like 'capitalised expenditure on development of new project'. This is fine and dandy as long as the new magazine produces the profits that are expected of it, and the capitalised expenditure can be written down in the balance sheet out of these profits as they begin to flow in. If the magazine turns out to be a flop, the capitalised expenditure shown in the balance sheet has no value and should be written off completely. Always have a close look at any capitalised expenditure that is carried forward in this way. It is not unknown for it to continue to appear in the balance sheet long after there is any realistic chance that it will be recouped from the profits of the project.

In the case of **WorldCom** in the United States, what appears to have happened is that almost $4bn that was really part of the operating expenses, and should have been deducted in arriving at the profits of the business, was treated instead as if it were investment in assets. In other words it was capitalised on the balance sheet. As a result, profits had been severely overstated.

The whole question of **capitalisation of costs** (particularly **interest costs**) is a thorny one and offers considerable scope for manipulation. This is one reason why you should look carefully at the note to the accounts that gives the detail of the year's interest charges. The problem is best explained with the example of a property investment and development company. This is a company that is in the business of developing new buildings (office blocks, say). When the building is finished the developer tries to find a tenant for it, then holds the finished office block as an investment for the rent it produces and for the future increase in its capital value.

To develop the new office block, our property company has to borrow money to cover the costs of buying the land and to pay for the construction work, etc. These **borrowings** are incurring interest charges from day one, but the project will not produce any income in the form of rent until it is completed and let, which could be a matter of several years. Should these interest costs be charged against the company's profits from other sources in the meantime, in which case published profits could be severely reduced? Or should they be treated as part of the capital cost of the new office block, in which case they are described as **capitalised**, and added in the balance sheet to all the other costs of the project like land purchase costs and construction costs?

If this second course is taken, the interest on the borrowings for the new project will not go through the profit and loss account and published profits will not therefore be damaged. But there is a danger. In the balance sheet the new office block will be shown during the construction period under fixed assets at what it has cost to date, including the **capitalised interest**. After it is completed and let it will be professionally revalued and will be shown at valuation from then on. The idea, naturally, is that the value of the offices should be considerably higher than what they cost, including the capitalised interest. The danger, however, was vividly demonstrated in the property market collapse of the early 1990s in Britain. If completion of the offices coincides with a time when tenants are difficult to find and values in the market have fallen, the offices may turn out to be worth less than they cost to construct, particularly where the costs have been inflated by large amounts of capitalised interest.

Where you are looking at property company accounts, one of the first things to check is whether interest is being capitalised or charged against the year's revenue (which is generally regarded as the more conservative course). It can make a massive difference to the look of the profit and loss account. And property is not the only asset on which interest may be capitalised. With any type of company you need to check whether any interest has been capitalised, see how this may have flattered the profit and loss account, and ask whether this risks inflating the cost of the asset beyond what it may be worth.

Questions about the accuracy of the figures at which assets are shown also crop up with **stocks**, shown under **current assets**. The basic rule is that stocks are shown at the lower of cost and net realisable value. In other words they will be shown at what they cost unless they are now worth less than this, in which case the values should be **written down**. The auditor of, say, a company making engineering parts was always supposed to damp his finger and run it along the top of the manufactured components in the trays where they were stored. If it came up with a lot of dust on it, this might suggest that the components had not been accessed for a long time and might therefore be obsolescent. In which case their value almost certainly needed writing down! Failure to write stocks down to their current worth is a common way of presenting a false picture in the balance sheet. If rag trade company

Payola Frocks misjudges the fashion trends and turns its production over to mini-skirts just before hemlines move down, the chances are that it is going to find itself with large quantities of virtually unsaleable stock. Has it come clean on this and written down the value of these stocks in the accounts? Unfortunately, sometimes not!

Stocks are the area of a company's accounts that offer the most scope for manipulation, particularly in a manufacturing company. The valuation of stocks may be treated in a number of different ways, and this can have direct implications for the profit shown in the profit and loss account, even where there is no intention to mislead. Thus, two otherwise identical companies could adopt different methods of **stock valuation** and come up with significantly different profit figures in a particular year as a result. This is because, although stocks are carried at the **lower of cost and net realisable value**, there is considerable latitude in the definition of 'cost'. In the case of semi-manufactured or finished goods, cost clearly includes the direct costs of the manufacturing process. But what other costs are included here? Is a proportion of group overheads and management costs included? The principles are defined in the Companies Act, but there is still inevitably a great deal of leeway. For example, a company that loaded all the costs it was legally allowed to onto its year-end stocks figure would in effect be carrying some of its expenditure in one year forward into the next year. This would benefit the first year's published profit at the expense of the profit of later years. This is one of the ways in which profits may be **smoothed** between years. Or, used to extremes, it could boost current profits way beyond the point at which they give a realistic view of the result of the company's operations. It really takes a qualified accountant to see the implications of any particular stock treatment. But even the general reader of accounts should be aware of the scope for manipulation.

The item that normally appears next to stocks under current assets – **debtors** – can also give a misleading impression. Normally, debtors are shown in the accounts net of a provision for **bad and doubtful debts**. When a company is effectively making loans to its customers in the form of **trade credit**, it knows there is a risk that some of them will fail to pay. So it may make provisions against specific debtors where it thinks there is a real risk of losing money on particular accounts or it may simply provide a percentage of its total debtors figure as a **bad debt provision**, to recognise the fact that it probably won't recoup absolutely everything that is owing to it. The problems usually crop up when a company has one particularly large customer that owes it a lot of money, and this customer gets into financial difficulties. Has our company written down its debtors figure in the accounts to recognise the strong likelihood that it will lose this money? If not, the accounts are giving a misleading impression. And the failure of a major customer can sometimes have a domino effect, with the company that had advanced trade credit to it suffering such a severe loss that it goes under itself.

A somewhat similar point crops up in the context of **contingent liabilities and guarantees**. These, remember, are liabilities that do not appear on the balance sheet because they are thought unlikely to materialise in practice. Has the company honestly disclosed all the possible contingent liabilities that it knows of? And is it right in its view that they are unlikely to arise in practice? If a company has given guarantees for very large **loans** made by banks to an **associated company**, it could find itself having to stump up if the associate hits financial difficulties and goes bust. And again the domino effect could come into play.

One of the other dodgy areas where accounts may give a misleading impression is in the use of **provisions** against future liabilities. As soon as a company knows that it faces a particular liability or loss in the future, which can be reasonably accurately quantified, it is required to make a provision against it. The provision will appear under **provision for liabilities and charges**. This used to be a fruitful area for accounts manipulation, but the **Accounting Standards Board** has now tightened up the position considerably. The provision has to be charged against the profit of the year in which it is made. And companies are no longer allowed to make provisions against trading losses expected in the future. But this still leaves some scope for manoeuvre.

Suppose a company plans to close down an unprofitable business division. Redundancy and other closure costs of £100m will be incurred, and the company is already legally committed to the closure plan. It makes a provision of £100m, which bashes the current year's profits. But over the next three years, say, when the costs are actually being incurred, there is no effect on the company's profit and loss account because the money has already been provided. The provision is gradually used up to meet the closure costs as they are incurred, but the only indication is likely to be in the note on provisions for liabilities and charges, which will show the amount of provisions used up during the year and the extent of any further provisions made. The result is that the company might have been forced to show a loss in the year in which it made the provision, even though it was trading profitably at the time. And in the years in which the closure is taking place, the company shows good profits even though these very large closure costs are being incurred at the time. In other words, the impact of events is being shifted from when they are actually taking place.

Companies, or those who run them, sometimes use this process to their advantage. A company has been in trouble for some time, say. A new chief executive is brought in who decides to perform radical surgery on the business by selling off underperforming parts at a loss and closing down various divisions at considerable cost in redundancies. At the same time he probably takes the opportunity to **write down** the value of various assets. His first year thus sees massive **provisions** to cover these costs and massive asset write-downs. As a result, the company is deeply loss-making after charging these one-off items in the profit and loss account. In other words, all the dirty linen is displayed in one single year. But in the subsequent years when these costs and losses are actually being incurred, the company starts publishing quite reasonable profits. The new chief executive is widely hailed in the press and elsewhere as a saviour. In reality, he may be, but he may not be. It's rather too early to tell from the published figures!

Two final areas which require a close look, particularly after the energy group **Enron** débâcle in America in 2001, are a company's use of **off balance sheet finance** and the extent of its trading with **related parties**. Both are areas where a number of abuses occurred in the past, though the British accounting rules in these areas have been tightened up considerably in recent years and such abuses are probably less likely in Britain today. In the case of Enron the company appeared to have traded extensively with companies which it did not technically control but which had close connections with Enron or its directors.

Off balance sheet financing describes a process whereby a company raises money via vehicles that are not technically part of the group and therefore these debts do not appear in its accounts. The way it might have worked in the past is this. Payola Properties plc is short of cash and so heavily borrowed already that it is unlikely to be able to raise further loans. So it gets an investment bank or similar institution to set up a company which is perhaps technically controlled by the bank. Payola has no shareholding in this company – call it NewCo – nor are any of its directors on the NewCo board. To all appearances, NewCo is a completely independent and unrelated company. Payola then sells some of its investment properties to NewCo for £100m, booking itself a £15m profit in the process which goes into its own profit and loss account. Newco pays for the properties by raising a £100m loan which is secured on them. Hasn't Payola lost control of its properties for good and forgone any chance of sharing in their future rise in value? Not a bit of it. There is some sort of option agreement or similar arrangement (the detail varied) whereby the properties could be sold back to Payola by NewCo for the same price at some time in the future. The effect of the transaction is that, in reality, Payola has sold properties to itself and booked a £15m profit in the process! It has effectively raised a £100m loan, but this loan will not have to appear on its balance sheet since the money was technically borrowed by NewCo. This sort of arrangement would be ruled out today by the changes in the accounting rules that we referred to. But no doubt clever accountants and lawyers have been beavering away at finding some loophole that could be exploited.

What can still be done in the UK is to use **associated companies** or **joint ventures** (companies owned fifty-fifty by two parties, but not controlled by either) to raise loans, which again do not need to be shown on the balance sheet of the part-owner. If the part-owner has given **guarantees** for these loans, it will have to say so. But a glance at its balance sheet will not show the total amount of debt to which it is exposed.

Under British accounting rules a company must disclose material dealings with **related parties**, a definition that covers its own directors and their immediate families or businesses in which they have a significant interest plus, of course, any business in which the company itself has an interest or where it exerts management influence. The amounts involved must be shown. Clearly, there could be suspicion that the transactions were not 'arm's length' and might therefore have favoured one party or another in a way that cast doubt on the accuracy of the profit figures shown. There is nothing necessarily wrong with transactions with related parties. They could be completely above board and undertaken on normal commercial terms. But it's nice to know about them all the same. And you would probably be more than a little worried if you found that 45% of the turnover of a listed company came from transactions with another company controlled by its chairman!

It was, incidentally, artificially inflated profits arising from dealings with related companies that brought the late Robert Maxwell into serious conflict with the stock exchange and takeover authorities way back in 1969. When Department of Trade Inspectors subsequently investigated what Maxwell had been up to, they came to the famous conclusion that 'he is not in our opinion a person who can be relied on to exercise proper stewardship of a publicly quoted company'. But the City of London has a short memory where it sniffs the opportunity of profit. In the 1980s Maxwell was being lauded again as a media mogul and publisher of the *Daily Mirror* newspaper. Banks were falling over themselves to lend to him. And Maxwell was embarking for a second time on a journey of fraud and deception that was going to lead to the plundering of pension funds and, arguably, to his own death.

What they really mean…

Company reports have a language of their own. The first principle is 'why use one word where five will do?' Why say 'We talk to trade unions' when you could say 'Appropriate consultative arrangements are in place to ensure that effective communication with employee representatives is maintained'? The second principle is to introduce impenetrable obscurity to even the simplest of concepts. You will frequently find statements on the following lines: 'A reduction in the strength of performance across a broad spectrum of our operating activities led to a deterioration in the contribution to the group from all our principal subsidiary undertakings with consequent failure to achieve our budgeted revenue objectives.' He probably means: 'We had a lousy year.'

Don't, of course, go away with the idea that chairmen write their statements themselves. What are public relations men and women for? So the chances are that a few fairly factual jottings from the great man have been turned at enormous expense into the weasel words that you will find in the published document. There's a fortune waiting for the first person who cuts out the cost of the human element (we are classifying public relations persons as human) by devising a computer program that will take plain English and turn it into the language of the annual report.

Computers are playing their part already. There are masses of statements on policy towards the disabled, the environment, directors' remuneration and the rest that any self-respecting lawyer, accountant or public relations person has safely stashed as 'boilerplate' text on his computer, ready to plonk into the next annual report that comes his way. Statements on these issues and many more are required by company law, the accounting rules or some code of corporate conduct. The idea is that it makes the directors at least briefly consider these issues once a year and put their name to a policy.

The computer has got round that one. The pre-packaged standardised statement on employment of the disabled can be dumped on the page without requiring consideration from anyone at all, let alone a director. It's a bit like that old definition of a university lecture: an event where words make their way from the notes of the lecturer to the notes of the students, without going through the minds of either. Observe, moreover, that companies always talk about their 'policy towards' the employment of the disabled. Have you ever come across a company that told you it employed disabled people, and how many? Readers of reports and accounts may be excused for skipping most of this guff altogether.

In fact, an essential art in reading a report and accounts is to know what is important and what isn't. What must be read and what can safely be ignored. But you have to be a little careful. Some companies are quite astute, when there is a bit of damaging information that they are required by law to impart, at tucking it away in the most unlikely places. The other essential art is learning to read between the lines. Below are some phrases of the type you might meet in a report and accounts, with a suggestion of what they might really mean. And before a libel lawyer lands on us from a great height, let us make it absolutely clear that we are not suggesting that any of these phrases has ever been used by any real company with the meaning we have attributed to it. Perish the thought.

'**This has been an excellent year for your company with pre-tax profits up by 55%.**' Well, an excellent year for the directors, whose bonuses are linked to pre-tax profits. Not so good for the shareholders, since earnings per share have fallen. The profits hike was entirely the result of a takeover for shares, at an inflated price!

'**Unfortunately, our widget division suffered very difficult trading conditions in the second half...**' Thanks to our failure to invest in new production plant, our competitors knocked the stuffing out of us in the widget market.

'**The restructuring and refocusing of your company continued during the past year, with renewed emphasis on our core business divisions.**' We've been flogging every saleable business to get our debt down and stave off insolvency. Keep your fingers crossed.

'**We are grateful for the support of our bankers during this very difficult period...**' We're bust, but the bank is propping us up for the moment in the hope of recovering some of its loans when it gets round to winding us up later, at its leisure.

'**Our most valuable resource is our skilled and loyal workforce...**' of which we have just sacked 40%, following the transfer of widget manufacture to Malaysia.

'**In accordance with the company's articles, our founder Kenneth Muckanbrass retires from executive office at the age of 75 but has agreed to accept the newly created office of President. We would like to pay tribute...**' At last! Now maybe we can get this show back on the road; possibly even install a computer or two!

'**The director of our Sicilian operations, Alfredo Scandaleoni, is retiring to devote more time to his family business interests.**' Nuff said.

'**Mission-critical logistical and symbiotic solutions for an increasingly homogeneous and demanding global customer base are now forming an increasing part of our business.**' Our new sanitary-ware range is selling well at home and overseas. And somebody's been spending too much time in the United States!

'**We always endeavour to continue to offer employment to members of our workforce who have met with disability during their employment with us.**' And a damn nuisance it is, too. Might be cheaper in the long run to get a guard fitted on that guillotine machine.

'**In our opinion the financial statements give a true and fair view...**' And we'd lose all that highly profitable consultancy work as well as the audit fee if we said that they didn't.

'**The group's policy is to consider the employment of disabled people where possible...**' Indeed, we do consider it every year. Haven't actually got one on the staff, of course.

'**Employee involvement is at the core of our business policy. Employees are kept informed of...**' We installed a Tannoy system on the shop floor.

'**Recommendations for new directors are made by the Remuneration and Nomination Committee.**' And with £20,000 a year as non-execs and an extra £7,000 for serving on the committee, its members know what's good for them. Must remind them my son's name comes up at the next meeting.

'**The company's remuneration policy is to provide competitive remuneration packages which enable the company to attract, motivate and retain executives of high calibre.**' And since every other company's bumping up its pay and perks packages to do exactly the same, boardroom pay continues to rise at about five times the rate of general wage inflation. But we're not complaining.

'**The company is an equal opportunities employer.**' We treat the *whole* of our workforce like dirt.

'**The inevitable redundancies forced upon us by adverse trading conditions will need to be spread across the board.**' No, not the board of directors, stupid! We've got three-year contracts!

'**We have considered it prudent in the light of current economic conditions to write down the value of intangible assets by 50%.**' Whose bright idea was it to bid for those new-generation mobile phone licences? And win one, dammit.

'**Our efforts have been focused on achieving greater public acceptance of the quality of our unique core product and our service to consumers.**' We've spent £5m on a new corporate logo and doubled our PR spend. Same lousy water out of the taps, though (when they work!).

'**Our corporate mission statement is...**' I've never felt quite right in the commercial world. Should have tried the church or the army instead.

'**Approaches have been received from a number of parties with a view to a takeover offer for your company, but none has so far...**' Negotiating my golden handshake is proving the stumbling block as usual.

'**We announced in November that there had been a breakdown in financial controls at our widget subsidiary and the share price fell as a result.**' Not half as far as it would have done if the full facts had got out.

'**In the light of the further bank facilities available to the group, the accounts have been prepared on a going concern basis.**' Going where? Shareholders should certainly feel concern.

'**Your company's long-term incentive plan for directors has been designed to align the interests of management and shareholders.**' Directors get their shares free, other shareholders pay for theirs. Shareholders lose real money when the share price falls. Directors don't.

'**We have continued to make progress with the integration of our recently acquired French subsidiary, Widgets SA, but profits to date have not met our original expectations...**' Damn Frenchies sold us a pup!

'**The operating culture of the group now embraces internal control and continuing assessment of risk...**' Previously, we crossed our fingers and hoped.

'**In the light of your company's financial structure and the known problems in the marketplace, future visibility is more than usually difficult.**' We're heading south fast and have no idea what to do about it.

'**Your board now consists of four executive directors and three non-executive directors, all of whom are independent.**' Except for the £40,000-odd each of them picks up for consultancy services to the group each year.

'**Frank Widget, who joined the board in April, brings to your company the wealth of knowledge and financial experience he acquired in his previous appointment with one of the world's largest international corporations.**' Pity it was Enron.

Index and glossary

This index and glossary lists the main pages where terms or concepts are explained or discussed in the text with the more important page references shown in **bold** type; it also provides explanations of some terms that do not crop up in the body of the text. Some terms such as 'profit' or 'asset' crop up so often that no attempt has been made to list every occurrence.

(for scrip issue)

equity, equities The term is used in a number of different senses. When used in a financial context **equity** normally means the ownership interest in an asset, subject to all the risks and rewards of ownership and after all other claims have been allowed for. If you have a house worth £200,000 subject to a mortgage of £130,000, your **equity interest** or **equity** in the house is £70,000. The **equity assets** of a company are what is left after all debts and claims (including those of preference shareholders) have been allowed for. In other words, they are what is attributable to the ordinary shareholders. **Ordinary shares** are called **equities** because they share fully in the risks and rewards of the business and are entitled to what is left after other claims have been met. The **debt/equity ratio** is the relationship between borrowed money and shareholders' money used in a business – i.e. the **gearing**. 52

ex-dividend, xd Dividends declared by a

W

warrants A conventional warrant is a bit like a traded option, though issued by the company rather than by an existing holder of the shares. The warrant entitles the holder to buy shares at some point in the future at a price determined when the warrant is issued. If the share price rises sufficiently to make it worth exercising the warrant by subscribing for the shares at this price, the company will normally create and supply the new shares required. Warrants may be traded in the stock market much like shares themselves.

wind up (a company) (*see* **liquidate**)

window dressing 153–154

work in progress (stocks) 16–17, 105

working capital 16, 18, 84–85, 140–141

WorldCom ix, 155–156

write down, written down, write off The values at which fixed assets appear in the accounts are written down, via the **depreciation** charge, to reflect their gradual wearing out. Fixed assets may also suffer a one-off write-down if something happens to **impair** their value permanently, so that they are no longer worth the figures shown in the books. Current assets will also sometimes need to be written down. In the case of **stocks** this would be because they could no longer be sold for the figures shown. **Debtors** may also need to be written down if it emerges that some of the money owing to the company is not recoverable. In extreme cases assets may need to be **written off** completely. 156

X

xc (*see* **ex-capitalisation**)

xd (*see* **ex-dividend**)

xr (*see* **ex-rights**)

Y

yield (*see* **dividend yield**)

About TEXERE

TEXERE seeks to become the most progressive and authoritative voice in business publishing by cultivating and enhancing ideas that will illuminate the global business landscape. Our name defines the spirit of our vision: TEXERE is the ancient Latin verb "to weave". In an increasingly global business community, we seek to create an intersection where authors and readers can share the best thinking and the latest ideas. We want to leverage the expertise and insights of leading thinkers by weaving them with TEXERE's capability to deliver them to the marketplace. To learn more and become a part of our community visit us at:

www.etexere.com
and
www.etexere.co.uk

About the typeface

This book was set in 10/12pt Friz Quadrata. Created by Swiss designer Ernst Friz, this typeface was released by the Visual Graphics Corporation in the late 1960s. The bold version was later added by Victor Caruso and the italic was added in the 1990s by Thierry Puyfoulhoux.